Robert Griffin

Challenger 1
Main Battle Tank
The Tankman's Experience Continues
vol. II

KAGERO

Introduction

The Challenger 1's service career started out with much publicity. Some readers will certainly agree that the Conservative government of the day ended up believing their own publicity, and this resulted in the Challenger's capabilities being overestimated just in time for the CAT87. The three years that followed CAT87 saw the Challenger under a dark cloud, and comprised a period when Britain's MBT was underestimated as an effective weapon system. It was not until early 1991 that the record was set straight about the Challenger 1. It was (by reason of its fire control system) not quite the super tank it could have been, but it was by sheer virtue of its firepower and protection, still one of the world's best in its day. Crewed by dedicated professionals, this was not proven in the artificial arena of gunnery competitions, but in the harsher world of the real battlefield.

Faith was restored in the Challenger 1 by Operation Granby, and the type served the Royal Armoured Corps for nearly another decade (often in harm's way) before being replaced by the Challenger 2. The Challenger 1 still serves the Jordanian armed forces as the Al Hussein and it will serve for years to come. In Volume 2 of Robert Griffin's Challenger 1 story from Kagero Publishing, the story is set out with a fine selection of photographs, many being from the collections of people who were there. The story of the CRARRV recovery vehicle is also included, along with a fine selection of colour plates showing the Challenger 1 gun tank's storied and continuing career.

M.P. Robinson, editor.

Test loading a Challenger on the landing ship Arromanches. [Brian Clark]

The Longcross test track at Chertsey Surrey was the scene of much of the Challenger's automotive testing in the early 1980s. [Brian Clark]

Challenger 1 Main Battle Tank. The Tankman's Experience Continues. Vol. II • Robert Griffin • First edition • LUBLIN 2014

 ISBN 978-83-64596-00-1

Editors: **M.P. Robinson, Tomasz Basarabowicz** • Photo credits: **The author would like to thank the following individuals and organizations for the use of their photos: John Cook, Dennis Lunn, Steve Harbord, Martin Jones, Martin Cassidy, Kim Hills, Phil Richards, Wayne Dunbar, David Brown, John 74, Steve Cleator, Phil Harvey, Neil Bolton, The British Army, MoD, Dave Thomas, Don Lawson, Derek Whitehouse, Royal Ordnance Factory, Plain Military (Andy Brend), Keith Frape, S. Park, Brian Clark, Malcolm Cleverley and of course Simon Dunstan. The editors would also like to personally thank Malcolm Cleverley, Dennis Lunn, John Rose, and Brian Clark for their help in this project.**

• Drawings in scales: **Piotr Boczoń**
• Design: **KAGERO STUDIO, Marcin Wachowicz, Łukasz Maj**

Oficyna Wydawnicza KAGERO
Akacjowa 100, Turka, os. Borek, 20-258 Lublin 62, Poland, phone/fax: (+48) 81 501 21 05
www.kagero.pl • e-mail: kagero@kagero.pl, marketing@kagero.pl
w w w . k a g e r o . p l
Distribution: **Oficyna Wydawnicza KAGERO**

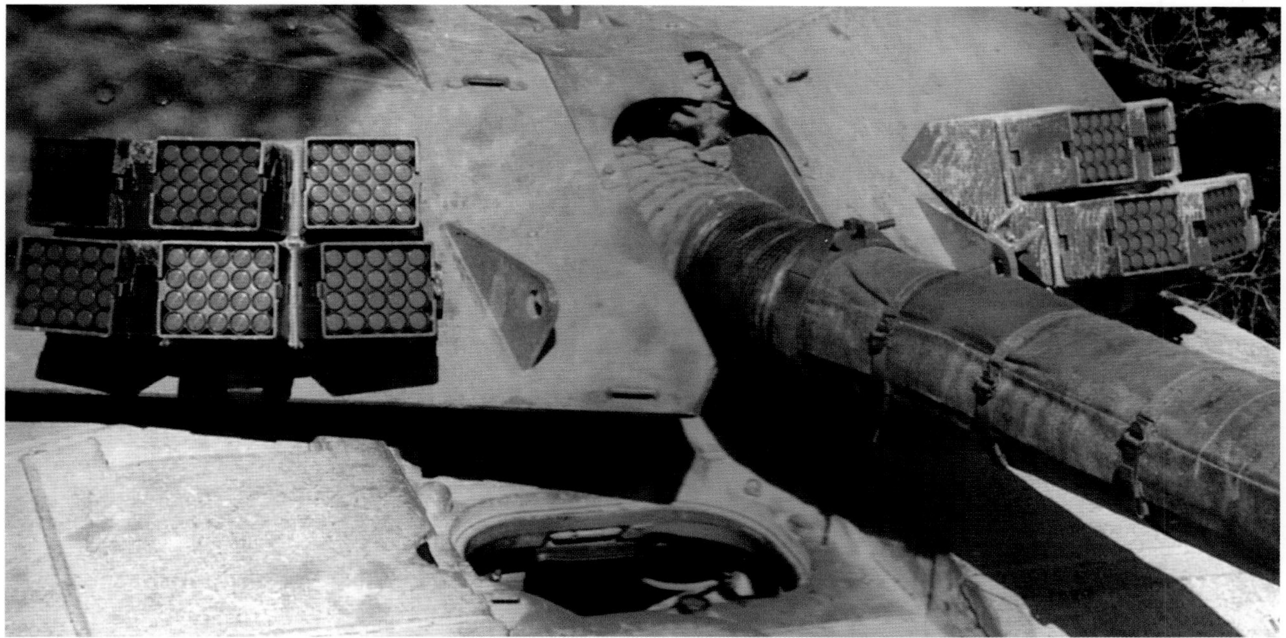

The standard smoke discharger fit adopted on the Challenger were not the only option considered during the Challenger's development. The visual infrared smoke discharger system was also considered for the Challenger and for the earlier Chieftain, but was never adopted. [RO]

The Challenger Enters Service

In 1985 the British Army had its new tank into service, although initially only 4 regiments would be equipped and the rest soldiered on with late model Chieftains. Although Challenger 1 was not perfect and still had faults, it was far better than the Chieftain especially in terms of protection and mobility. The Challenger was accepted with some acclaim in the press too, for naturally it was seen as a job saver for ROF Leeds' large workforce and also as a natural successor to the already potently armed Chieftain. The optimism the new tank was accepted with was short-sighted because it had one large failing that would limit the Challenger in many eyes to mediocrity amongst its shining peers, the M1 and Leopard 2.

Like Chieftain before it, Challenger 1 was of interest to the armies of many nations, but sadly the expected sales did not ensue. It may be said that Royal Ordnance PLC and Vickers in years afterwards, were poor tank salesmen. One nation with an interest in the Challenger at the time of its introduction was Egypt, and as a result of a meeting held in the United Kingdom between Lieutenant-General El Orabi (the Chief of Staff of the Egyptian Armed Forces) and the British Ministry of Defence, it was agreed that Challenger 1 should be put through a series of trials for the Egyptian Armoured Corps,as requested by the Egyptians. The trials were to take place early in the United Kingdom in December 1985, after the type had been in regimental service in the Royal Armoured corps for nearly 18 months.

The trial would consist of three phases:

Phase 1: Automotive and Maintenance phase at R.A.C. Centre Bovington.

Phase 2: Gunnery Phase- R.A.C. Ranges Kirkcudbright.

Phase 3: Automotive Running and Obstacle Crossing Phase- Catterick Garrison.

The automotive phase at Bovington was marred by heavy rainfall, making the cross country course heavy with mud and large puddles, so the trial committee agreed that the trial should

The Challenger prototypes were used for demonstrations and development work during the early days of the Challenger 1s service. [RO]

to 1st BRITISH CORPS

1st ARMOURED DIVISION

1st BRITISH CORPS

7th ARMOURED BRIGADE

23rd JUNE 1983 BERGEN HOHNE

Cover page of a pamphlet issued when the Challenger was officially presented to BAOR at Bergen Hohne in late June 1983. [John Cook]

be a 50/50 split between cross country and road operation. Due to the conditions on the cross country track the actual split ended up as a 37/63 split; but this portion of the trial was deemed a success with the Challenger performing as per the trial requirements, and only normal operational maintenance tasks were required to keep the tank operational. While the automotive trial was running, the members of the Egyptian military delegation were given constant updates and briefings as to what was going on.

The gunnery phase of the trial was designed to show the Egyptian team the accuracy and effectiveness of the L11A5 gun and the standard ammunition types used. The ammunition natures employed consisted of HESH (High Explosive Squash Head), APDS (Armour Piercing Discarding Sabot), APFSDS (Armour Piercing Fin Stabilised Discarding Sabot) and SH/PRAC (Squash Head Practice). These were to be fired from a static vehicle engaging static targets, then from a static vehicle engaging moving targets and finally from a moving vehicle engaging moving targets. The engagement sequences were also designed to show how the trunnion tilt compensator in the gunner's sight could compensate for the tank's armament being fired on a side slope. Weather-related problems beset the gunnery phase, including the cancellation of a night firing sequences, all of which would not seem to indicate that the Challenger was an all-weather weapon system capable of operating 24 hours a day. One would wonder if the Egyptians had developed misgivings by this stage. The coaxial machine gun and smoke discharger drills were not demonstrated either.

A crew from the R.A.C. fired most of the practice engagements for the trial although an Egyptian gunner did fire some

With the regimental band playing and with the new tanks carefully marked with the Royal Hussars crest, one can sense the high expectations the army had for the Challenger MBT. [John Cook]

Royal Ordnance and the Royal Hussars during the handover ceremony. [John Cook]

of the serials. The DS/T firing involved firing eighty rounds at fixed and moving targets, at ranges up to 2500m the hit rate was 92.5%; the rate against a moving target was astonishingly 100% and 85% was achieved from a moving tank against a moving target. The firing of APFSDS munitions gave acceptable accuracy

The early days of the Challenger's entry into service with the Royal Hussars were accompanied by the technical difficulties typical of a new weapon's introduction to service. [John Cook]

scores but the main issue was that despite the grouping of the rounds fired being very close, the actual mean point of impact was very low on the target. It was accepted that the grouping did show how accurate the L11 gun was. The SH/PRAC firing trials had a very bad start, firing twenty eight rounds- and scoring no hits, which caused consternation. The ammunition batch was withdrawn and deemed faulty. With a new batch of ammunition things improved and the hit rate was deemed acceptable, but first impressions may have counted. The R.A.C. crew showed that it was possible to load with the standard separate bagged charge ammunition at a commendable rate of 8 rounds a minute consistently. Two serials fired by the visiting Egyptian gunner both had a 100% hit rate.

The final automotive phase then took place at Catterick Garrison in North Yorkshire, and was designed to show the Challenger's impressive obstacle crossing capability; but looking at the report results, the course chosen seems to have been uninspired. The Challenger crossed a series of obstacles which did not trouble it, having crossed more arduous ones during

The regiment received a steady stream of visitors, and the regiment was expected to showcase the new tank for the government's benefit. [John Cook]

The Royal Hussars on parade in the 1984-1986 period with Challengers lined up in the background. [John Cook]

A Royal Hussars crew being inspected in the early days of the Challenger's service with the regiment. [John Cook]

A serious looking Challenger driver in the head out driving position. [John Cook]

a demonstration in the Middle East earlier in the year. That concluded the trials and although the hospitality must have been laid on thickly, the actual sequence of events (one would suspect) probably did not impress the visitors. Cancelling trials for bad weather seems irregular, and foolish in light of the need to prove a weapon's capabilities...which along with the accuracy issues with the practice ammunition probably made the Egyptians decide against buying the Challenger 1. It would not be last time Vickers bungled its chances of selling a British tank.

The Challenger's first real test in British hands was waiting in the form of the NATO tank gunnery competition known as the Canadian Army Trophy (CAT) and the end result would be a scandal. The Royal Armoured Corps was keen to restore its pride after the Royal Scots Dragoon Guards had come last in CAT 85 equipped with the Chieftain, so CAT87 was seen as the perfect opportunity to "sell" the Challenger. Sadly all did not go to plan. Much has been written about the actual event and space precludes a full write up here (an excellent account is available in the Osprey New Vanguard on Challenger 1 by Simon Dunstan), so suffice it to say that the Challenger came a very poor last in the event and of the many myths that have grown around it, some have some basis in truth.

Amongst the first things a regiment re-equipping with new tanks is eager to determine is how they will perform on the ranges. Because the Challenger carried on the proven technology of the Chieftain, most of its turret systems were familiar to experienced crews. Here we can see the L11A5 120mm gun at full depression and the co-axial machine gun. [John Cook]

Although the Challenger hit more targets than most during its battle run, its engagement times were painfully slow compared to the hunter-killer equipped Leopards and Abrams. The slow engagement times were blamed by many in the defence press on the 3-piece ammunition the British used, but in reality the problems were centered on the IFCS system and the turret's poor ergonomics. In essence the Challenger was the wrong tank at the wrong time, trying to win a competition against tanks equipped with stabilised gunnery sights and panoramic commander's sights. The Challenger went to CAT 87 using more or less the same fire control system as Chieftain had before it due to its Shir 2 lineage, the commanders sights on the Challenger

Call sign 41, B Squadron RH, being bombed up with the large 120mm HESH rounds. The crews wear DPM combat jackets over their tank suits. [John Cook]

Call sign 10, C Squadron RH, a moment after firing. The range flag is visible to the right of the commander's cupola. Note the prominent slope downwards from the cupola towards the loader's side of the Challenger's turret roof, not as visible from the front view. [John Cook]

had been tweaked to try and help it in the competition: but with sights only stabilised in two axes it was never going to win.

One innovation arising from the run up to CAT 87 that proved successful (and has carried over to Challenger 2) was the fitting of the "Chase Modification"; this was invented by S/Sgt Charlie Chase of the 4th/7th Royal Dragoon Guards, and was simplicity in itself. Chase modified the breech closing mechanism to work so that when the loader completed his last part of loading (pulling the breech safety guard to the rear) this closed the breech. Prior to this the loader would have to close the breech using the breech closing lever after engaging the safety guard. The new method was faster and worked very well, but

Call sign 42, B Squadron the Royal Hussars on the ranges sometime in the 1983-1986 period. [John Cook]

Two troops worth of Royal Hussars Challengers deploying in West Germany, in another photo taken by the regimental photographer prior to 1986. [John Cook]

A colour photo shot in the mid-1980s of a B Squadron, Royal Hussars Challenger on exercise. Note how the smoke dischargers are uncovered, indicating that they have been fired. [John Cook]

A Challenger 1 of the Royal Hussars rumbles past a line of Thornycroft Antar tank transporters in West Germany. [John Cook]

A frosty looking day in the mid-1980s in BAOR, two B Squadron Challengers of the Royal Hussars. [John Cook]

These Challengers are probably preparing for a range period. The Challenger in the background is a squadron command tank, which had a different wireless fit. [John Cook]

A dusty and appropriately marked Royal Hussars Challenger seen here in a publicity shot taken by the regimental photographer in the mid-1980s. [John Cook]

it would take vision devices of the order initially envisioned for MBT 80 to have rectified the weaknesses exposed in the Challenger's fire control system by CAT 87.

The sensationalist British press of course had field day, as did the armchair experts in the defence press. The author can recall being in the RAC Centre just after the CAT87 shoot and listening to people saying "never mind politics, let's just buy the Abrams", but these were not ordinary soldiers voicing this opinion. Sales of the Challenger were doomed from the end of CAT 87 and the government were quickly forced to reappraise the domestic MBT program. In the RAC however life had to go on, the Challenger was still new and deliveries continued: 1985 had seen the 16 remaining Royal Ordnance Factories privatised into Royal Ordnance PLC, from whom Vickers purchased ROF Leeds in 1986. Vickers were still committed to existing contracts, so purchasing a new tank from a UK supplier was not an

This very soberly marked Challenger was probably photographed a few years later, but is also from the Royal Hussars. [John Cook]

Here is an interesting photo of a Challenger with mismatched skirting plates. [John Cook]

Here we see 06 SP 42, a later prototype. Some of the prototypes endured as test vehicles and as sales platforms for Royal Ordnance for a few years in the mid 1980s. [John Cook]

An early Challenger, probably from the Royal Hussars, in the mid 1980s. [John Cook]

This Royal Hussars Challenger is fitted with a Simfire system for simulated combat. The Simfire system was a training tool that was employed for many years in several variants with considerable success. [John Cook]

A Challenger rumbles out of its garage, 34 KA 00, of the Royal Hussars. The crew are wearing their bone domes. The Bone Dome was inherited from the Chieftain and was not universally liked by British tank crews due to its bulk. [John Cook]

option in the 1987-88 timeframe (and buying abroad was not an option considered politically acceptable). While the Ministry of Defence saw the need to replace the Challenger as well as the Chieftain in the long term, it would have to bide its time and make use of the Challenger.

During the 1985-87 period the RAC had to soldier on with two very different tanks, which did not save money as hoped, but actually increased spending because the logistics were complicated by having to maintain two different sets of spares in the supply chain. Eventually in 1988 the government had to concede that a new MBT to replace the rest of the Chieftain fleet was required, and a competition was set up using versions of M1 Abrams, Leopard 2, a new Vickers project tentatively named Challenger 2 and later the French Leclerc, to see which would satisfy the new General Staff Requirement 4026 *Chieftain Replacement Program*. While the Leopard 2 and M1A1 were both trialled for the requirement the political intent was to keep the new MBT British.

On the 20 December 1988 at 15:32 the then Secretary of State for Defence made the following announcement "After

Here we can see 34 KA 00 at rest, its crew now bareheaded. [John Cook]

Old and new: a brand new Challenger and a Royal Hussar in ceremonial dress. All the old cavalry regiments in the Royal Armoured Corps had lineages stretching back for generations. Even though rounds of amalgamations had taken place several times during the Cold War, tradition always held an important place in the esprit de corps of the regiments of the RAC. [John Cook]

On the ranges at night with Challengers of the Royal Hussars. [John Cook]

Spectacular photo of a range period at night with the Royal Hussars in the mid-1980s. [John Cook]

the most careful consideration I have decided to give Vickers Defence Systems an opportunity to demonstrate that it is able to deliver Challenger 2 to specification, to time and cost. Subject to satisfactory contract terms the government will fund a development phase which will last until September 1990 when the final decision will be made. While this was good news for

After 6 tries this Challenger of the Royal Hussars managed to climb correctly aboard the trailer of this Scammel Commander, perhaps a testament to the new tank's larger size versus the older and more familiar Chieftain. The Commander gradually replaced the Thorneycroft Antar as the standard tank transporter in the 1980s. [Malcolm Cleverley]

CANADIAN ARMY TROPHY 1987 MASTER SCOREBOARD

	PLATOON		HIT SCORE	TIME SCORE	AMMO BONUS	HIT BONUS	MG SCORE	TTKEF PENALTY	PLATOON TOTAL	TEAM TOTAL	REMARKS
NORTHAG	1 Royal Husars	UK	9166	5440			2000	13,41	16606	16606	22 of 24 (reru
	2 PzBtl 324	GE	9062	5610			2000	12,19	16672	33278	29 of 32
	3 43 Tkbat	NL	9375	6885			2000	6,72	18260	51538	30 of 32
	4 2-66 Armor	US	9062	6290			2000.	12,11	17352	68890	29 of 32
	5 4 Lanciers	BE	9062	5610			1750	12,19	16422	85312	29 of 32
	6 2-66 Armor	US	9062	6290			2000	8,66	17352	102844	29 of 32
	7 43 Tkbat	NL	8750	5865			1750	9,83	(16365)	120376	28 of 32
	8 PzBtl 324	GE	8750	5695			2000	10,79	16445	136741	28 of 32
	9 Royal Husars	UK	7083	4590			2000	11,20	13673	150414	17 of 24
	10 2-66 Armor	US	8750	6375			2000	7.09	17125	167539	28 of 32
	11 4 Lanciers	BE	9375	6325			2000	8.53	17700	185239	30 of 32
	12 Royal Husars	UK	7916	4590			1800	14,23	14306	199545	19 Of 24
re-run	Royal Husars		7500	4760			2000	11,73	14260	195727	18 of 24
CENTAG	1 3-64 Armor	US	9062	5780			1950	11,31	16792	16792	29 of 32
	2 4-8 Cav	US	8750	6205			1975	8,06	16930	33722	28 of 32
	3 RC Dragoons	CA	9062	6120			1975	9,54	17175	50879	29 of 32
	4 PzBtl 124	GE	9687	6035			2000	11,92	17722	68601	31 of 32
	5 PzBtl 363	GE	9375	6035			2000	10,09	17410	86011	30 of 32
	6 R C Dragoons	CA	9687	6375			2000	9.37	18062	102761	31 of 32
	7 3-64 Armor	US	8750	5950			2000	10,27	16700	120823	28 of 32
	8 4-8 Cav	US	9375	6630			2000	8,00	18005	138828	30 of 32
	9 PzBtl 363	GE	9687	6970			2000	7,78	18657	157485	31 of 32
	10 PzBtl 124	GE	10000	6715	500	500	1975	9,60	19690	177175	32 of 32
	11 3-64 Armor	US	9687	7140			2000	6,55	18827	196002	31 of 32
	12 4-8 Cav	US	10000	7165	800	500	1925	7,48	20490	216492	32 of 32

The scores at CAT87, where the Royal Hussars competed against a host of top teams from other NATO armies. In competition against West German and American-built MBTs, the Challenger scored poorly, causing a scandal. [R. Griffin]

Seen in the environs of the Royal Armoured Corps Centre Bovington, Challengers from 3rd RTR return from a morning of training in the late 1980s. [Malcolm Cleverley]

The 2nd RTR was another Challenger unit, and was one of the two regiments which were nominated to train for CAT87. This camouflaged Challenger was photographed on exercise. [Steve Harbord]

Another 3rd RTR Challenger raising dust on the training area at Bovington. [Malcolm Cleverley]

Vickers the Americans and Germans felt they had been cheated (Leclerc was never a serious contender, not because it was a poor tank but simply because its crew of 3 men was not to UK requirements). While the Challenger 2 held great promise the intended fleet would be a mix of both Challengers 1 and Challenger 2, again a bit of a fudge. The collapse of the Warsaw Pact in 1989 very quickly put the Challenger 1's future in doubt and caused a reappraisal of how many tanks were needed in BAOR in short order.

Operation Granby

World events were again about to step in and alter many things because in August 1990 Saddam Hussein invaded Kuwait, and as part of the international effort to remove him the UK initially deployed 7th Armoured Brigade (initially under US command) then deployed the entire 1st UK Armoured Division (comprised of the 7th Armoured Brigade and the 4th Mechanized Brigade, which arrived in December 1990 in-theatre) to the Persian Gulf. The Operation Granby deployment would eventually number 43,000 men in the largest army deployment since the Second World War. Much like the Falklands Campaign of 1982, it showed up errors and weaknesses in British operational capabilities. Two of 7th Armoured Brigade's Armoured

This 2nd RTR Challenger was photographed advancing down a road on a training area, probably in the late 1980s. [Steve Harbord]

With a green range flag flying, this 2nd RTR Challenger 1 was photographed on the firing ranges, perhaps at Bergen-Hohne. [Steve Harbord]

Regiments (The Royal Scots Dragoon Guards and The Queens Royal Irish Hussars), both equipped with Challenger 1, were dispatched to Saudi Arabia in September 1990 while the coalition assembled.

The 7th Armoured Brigade deployed both the QRIH and SCOTS DG as reinforced regiments with 57 Challenger 1s each supplemented with a full 14 tank squadron attached from the 17/21st Lancers and with a reinforcement pool of 43 more Challenger 1s drawn from The Life Guards available to replace any battle casualties. The infantry component was provided by the 1st Battalion The Staffordshire Regiment in 45 Warrior Mechanized Infantry Combat Vehicles. The 4th Mechanized Brigade included the 14/20th Hussars with 57 Challenger 1s reinforced with a full squadron of The Life Guards with an additional 14 Challenger 1s. These tanks were deployed in battle groups with the 1st Battalion Royal Scots and 3rd Battalion Royal Regiment of Fusiliers each with 45 Warrior Mechanized Infantry Fighting Vehicles.

A Challenger recovery in process at BATUS in Canada, early 1990s. [Steve Harbord]

A 2nd RTR Challenger photographed from the rear. The white ring markings on the barrel were a 2nd RTR marking. [Steve Harbord]

The angular lines of the Challenger 1 were a consequence of the use of Chobham armour. The Challenger looked every inch the epitome of a modern Main Battle Tank. The older fire control system the Challenger had inherited from the Chieftain was not apparent to the untrained eye, and when CAT-87 proved a bitter experience for the British team, many in the defence press simply wrote the Challenger off. The Challenger was however, later proved to be an excellent combat vehicle. This 2nd RTR Challenger was photographed during training in West Germany. [Steve Harbord]

The Challenger, like the Chieftain before it, wore large call signs and zap codes on the Alberta plain at Suffield. [Steve Harbord]

The Challenger Marksman was an anti-aircraft tank briefly marketed as an option by a consortium including Royal Ordnance and Marconi. The Marksman turret was a modular unit that could be fitted to a wide range of hulls, including the T54/55/59/62, T72, AMX-30, Centurion, Chieftain and M60 series to name a few. Nobody bought the Challenger Marksman, which was aimed squarely at the British Army, who had not used a dedicated AA tanks since the Crusader and Centaur AA tanks of 1944-1945, and had already ordered the Tracked Rapier AA missile system. [RO]

On arrival in the Persian Gulf a major training program was instigated, firstly to acclimatise the crews to the desert and working on tanks in the heat. After some weeks of guarding the Saudi border with few modifications other than sand coloured paint, the second other major issue was the decision to upgrade the armour package and navigation equipment on the Challenger to better suit local threats expected during the invasion of Kuwait. In addition to older and modern MBT's, the Iraqi Army deployed large numbers of Soviet and Chinese made ATGMs and infantry weapons of the RPG family. Additional armour would be made available for nearly every tank in theatre to protect the men and machines from all possible threats. All the armoured units that took part in Operation Granby (the UK name for Gulf War) used the Challenger 1 Mk3 or modified Challenger Mk.2 to Mk.3 standard, incorporating armoured charge bins instead of the charge bins surrounded by water jackets.

BAOR had never maintained sufficient spares to deploy the Challenger out of theater, which was made embarassingly clear at the beginning of Operation Granby in September 1990. To ensure that the 1st UK Armoured Division had enough spares for such a large operation in harsh conditions, spares were stripped from all available Challenger Mk.3s and most of the Mk.2 fleet in BAOR. [Crown Copyright]

The Challenger force was heavily supported by the defence industry for deployment to the gulf (at least 210 MBT's were sent, out of 420 available Challenger 1's. These included nearly all available Mk3 and upgraded Mk2 vehicles, while the remainder in BAOR were stripped for spare power packs and road wheels). With the thaw in East-West relations the availability rate for Challenger 1 by 1990 had been allowed to drop as low as 23% in BAOR in an effort to minimise wear and to keep fuel and maintenance costs as low as possible. This demanded immediate rectification for deployment overseas and showed BAOR logistics and rapid deployment planning in a very poor light that smacked of complacency. The gulf environment presented different operational and tactical problems than combat in northwest Europe, and this was reflected in the series of in-theatre upgrades performed by Vickers and other defence industry companies to ensure Challenger was as well protected as possible with both passive and reactive armour packages.

The ROMOR reactive armour upgrade added to the Challenger's lower front plate consisted of a carrier fixed to the toe

Challenger call sign 40 of the SCOTS DG advancing during Operation Granby. [Academic Dictionary]

A Challenger followed by a CRARRV during the advance into Iraqi held Kuwait in 1991. The Challenger is carrying a fair amount of stowage strapped to its side arrays, impossible in Europe but almost universal in the desert. [Trevor Gray]

The crew of call-sign 41 from A Squadron, Royal Scots Dragoon Guards, taking a break during their preparations for the push into Kuwait, notice how the tank stowage of a vehicle in action has a cluttered look to it. As funny as it sounds, each crew member will know exactly where every item is stowed. [P.C.Holmes]

A view of the very featureless terrain that Challenger 1 and the coalition forces would be fighting over during the liberation of Kuwait in 1991. Operating in the desert meant a whole new raft of skills had to be learnt, especially in the art of desert navigation. Very distinctive for the Challenger are the twin plumes of black smoke that exit from the exhaust once revolutions are applied to the power pack, still not as profuse as the clouds of white smoke that would often follow the Chieftain. [DW]

Kuwait, 1991: a good sort-out, possibly after the ground war was over. Notice the sleeping bags hanging over the gun barrel and road wheels lying to the rear of the vehicle. A section of the side appliqué armour is missing at the rear. The crewman on the ground has the tank petrol cooker out, and is trying to light up in order to cook some food. [Trevor Gray]

Three Challengers adopting a temporary defensive position during the training for the ground war prior to Operation Granby in 1990. Since there is no threat, all three have their turrets trained to the rear. [DL]

plate of the tank, into which ERA blocks were fitted. This was the only part of the frontal armour not fitted with Chobham armour, with rolled homogenous steel armour only 70mm thick, for the Challenger's armour layout had been optimised to fight hull-down. The vehicle sides were protected with large panels of Chobham armour as extra side skirts (because the basic Challenger 1 was equipped only frontally with Chobham armour). Other work went on to modify the engine systems for desert operations, all of which was rather ironic as Challenger was born of a tank designed for desert use, brought into service

The Black Jerboa insignia of the 4th Mechanised Brigade during Operation Granby; also on the front of the TOGS barbette is the insignia of the 20th Hussars, indicating a tank of the 14/20th Hussars. [DL]

Another view of the TOGS barbette on one of the 14/20th Hussars' Challengers after Operation Granby. [DL]

It seems like the crew of this Challenger have followed in the footsteps of aircraft crews (and some of the US Shermans from the Korea War era] in decorating the bow armour with large fearsome teeth. [DL]

to fight on the European plains and finally going to war in the desert. During the build-up from September 1990 onwards the dramatic reliability improvement seen in the Challenger fleet was due in no small way to the efforts of many of the contractors who sent teams to support the effort; these included: Vickers Defence Systems, David Brown, Barr and Stroud and Perkins (although many others were involved). All this did give Challenger a boost in the UK press, but the provision of spares for Operation Granby came at a cost. Many of the papers also published pictures of the remaining Challenger fleet back in BAOR with tanks jacked up onto stands and all automotive assembly's and suspension units removed and sent to the Gulf.

Due to a lack of spares and logistics personnel, BAOR had no real armour available for the period of the Gulf War, which

Loading a Challenger onto a Scamell Commander tank transporter for transport back to the docks, after the end of Operation Granby. Notice the angle the tank reaches before coming down onto the deck of the transporter. A good view of the tank's bottom plate shows the castellated reinforcing strip that joins both hull plates, seen on all of Challenger's plate joints. [DL]

A line up of war weary Challengers after the end of the ground war in Kuwait. They have been stripped of all crew kit and would appear to be getting ready for shipment back to either BAOR or the U.K., these vehicles belong to the Queens Royal Irish Hussars of the 7th Armoured Brigade as can be evidenced by the name Aughnacloy, a town in Northern Ireland, on the very right hand tank. [DL]

These 1st Armoured Division Challenger 1s have yet to receive their appliqué armour but are undergoing the first stage of upgrades, which included system checks. The turret systems and in particular the TOGS system so vital to the Challenger's ability to fight in low visibility and at night were very carefully checked over by defence industry representatives in the weeks before the ground offensive began. The tank in the foreground is undergoing an inspection on its TOGS system. [DL]

Freshly arrived at the docks a Challenger 1 and CRAARV line up awaiting their crew. Ingenious as always, the crews have made a shelter from the sun using two camp beds. Notice the kit strewn around waiting to be stowed on the tanks. [DL]

The fate of another Iraqi tank; these out-dated Russian T55s and Chinese copies (T59/T69) stood no chance against the modern armour employed by the coalition. [PW]

Close up of a Challenger off-loading from the Commander tank transporter. These huge vehicles were used to save wear and tear on the main battle tanks and to reduce the track mileage before the actual ground war to liberate Kuwait started. [DL]

Scamell Commander unloading a Challenger after bringing it from the docks, notice the transporter crewman guiding the tank back from the transporter. Most of the time, when loading and unloading, the tank driver is virtually blind and depends on the hand signals from the transporter crew. [DL]

A good rear shot showing the method to tie down the tank once on the transporter, the brackets for holding the long range fuel drums are pictured holding little 25 litre engine oil drums. [DL]

is a damming indictment of the supply chain and to some extent of the reliability of Challenger. It would be rectified in the months that followed Operation Granby, but it also illustrated how difficult it would be for Britain to deploy such a large force outside the NATO zone and simultaneously meet NATO commitments. These factors were heavily re-examined in the years that followed Operation Granby as British foreign policy closely followed that of its principal ally, the USA, and while it shrunk the commitment to German bases to the point of eventually replacing BAOR entirely with the much smaller BFG (British Forces Germany) in 1994.

Along with the armour upgrades, Operation Granby Challengers were fitted with a smoke generator system provided by injecting fuel into the hot exhaust and the fitting of 45 gallon drums at the rear for extra fuel (for a daily range of approximately 245 km). The Challenger's anti-tank capabilities were also upgraded. The biggest worry to the British was a Challenger versus T-72 battle (the T-72 being a known threat to prior

This shows just how near the ground the rear of the tank gets when offloading from the transporter. At one point the sprocket is actually on the ground itself, and this is why great care must be taken loading and unloading a tank. [DL]

On the docks, newly arrived Challenger 1 Mk.3s prepare to move off to their assembly area. [DL]

A rear three quarter view of a Challenger 1 in the gulf showing the rear fuel drum mounts and the side armour arrays. The fuel drums are in a brick reddish colour, and were seen in several different colours during the campaign. [DL]

A soberly painted Challenger 1 Mk.3 fitted with the side armour arrays awaits issue back to its unit at the beginning 1991. [DL]

This is most likely a SCOTS DG Challenger 1 Mk.3 from 7th Armoured Brigade at the end of 1990, as the coalition forces gathered. [DL]

designs like the Chieftain, and its current potential capabilities being relatively unknown to the British, who had never before fought it), so to give the Challenger the edge a program called Operation Jericho was put into place. This involved providing each Challenger with 12 Depleted Uranium L26A1 APFSDS rounds and the improved bagged charge to go with them (the L41A1), and it was stressed to crews that these rounds were only to be used against T-72.

On the 25th February 1991 the waiting was over, and the British 1st Armoured Division crossed the mine breach and headed into Kuwait, the crews were still wearing their chemical warfare suits as it was still believed that Saddam would employ chemical agents as a last resort against the coalition. The armoured regiments of the 1st Armoured Division were handled aggressively and immediately engaged the Iraqi forces wherever they were encountered. Both the SCOTS DG and the

A line of Challengers about to be upgraded for the ground offensive. [DL]

This lineup of Challenger 1 Mk.3s awaits the fitting of ROMOR reactive armour, Chobham side arrays and long range fuel drums. [DL]

This tank is part way through the up-armouring process and is waiting for its ROMOR pack. [DL]

A break during the up-armouring process at the end of 1990. The spaced armour plate is fitted to this tank's glacis, and the REME men were starting to fix the Chobham armour packs into frames on the tank's side when the tea break bell rang. [DL]

On the ranges. After CAT87 one of the things that the Granby Challenger crews were quite happy to show off was their prowess at gunnery. The longest kill shot recorded by a tank was made a few weeks later by a Challenger. [DL]

This is possibly a QRIH camp in the 7th Armoured Brigade sector during Operation Granby, it is striking how vast and featureless the terrain was during the liberation of Kuwait. The QRIH wore black call signs but also had a squadron of the 17/21st Lancers under command for the campaign. [DL]

QRIH had officers and men decorated for their bravery and professionalism in combat with the Challenger, but overall the invasion was a very unequal affair with British and American technology far outweighing the capabilities of Saddam's army's Soviet and Chinese equipment. The Challenger confounded its critics by performing exactly as it had been designed to, demonstrating an excellent reliability record and awesome firepower. The 4th Mechanized Brigade and 7th Armoured Brigade ran up a tally of over 300 enemy tanks destroyed without the loss of a single Challenger. While only T-55 series MBT's and

These Challengers, asides from the extemporised stowage rigged up from Chieftain stowage bins and empty ammunition boxes, are pretty much stock BAOR Challengers painted in desert sand. With the Scottish flag flying, they are the Royal Scots Dragoon Guards (always abbreviated to SCOTS DG]. This photo was taken in the last weeks of 1990, and the tanks are waiting to be fitted with their ROMOR and Chobham side armour kits. [DL]

These are probably the Queen's Royal Irish Hussars' vehicles waiting their turn to be fitted with the add-on armour and long range fuel drums, Ferret scout car stowage bins have been fitted to the right side of the turret as extra stowage on both vehicles. [DL]

A desert campsite somewhere in the 7th Armoured Brigade area in late 1990. [DL]

derivatives were encountered, the 4th Mechanised and 7th Armoured Brigade battle groups had demonstrated their expertise in long range gunnery engagements. Operation Jericho had proved quite unnecessary and overestimated the capabilities of the T-72. In every encounter between the American M1A1 and T72, the Soviet tank had been utterly beaten by the American tank's armour and gun. In the event the Challenger versus T-72 battles never took place, and going by the performance of the US M1A1 with very similar anti-tank capabilities and protection levels to the British tank, the Challenger 1 would have been perfectly adequate to deal with Iraqi T-72s at all combat ranges. Erring on the side of caution, it is evident that the Challenger 1 would have been perfectly capable of destroying the T-72 with normal ammunition well beyond the ranges where T-72 could have posed any threat and the Challenger's frontal protection would have been perfectly adequate against the T-72's 125mm gun. The Challenger's IFCS system despised in the CAT87 competition was also found to be superior to that fitted in any Iraqi MBT.

Some interesting points arose from the desert combat and were highlighted by Major General Patrick Cordingly (commander of 7th Armoured Brigade), one of which was the use of HESH as the ready round. It had been standard operating procedure in BAOR for MBTs to travel with a round loaded, and as per BAOR doctrine this was always a kinetic energy round. In Operation Granby it was found that APFSDS was overkill for light armour targets and would pass right through light AFVs, whereas HESH did serious initial damage to any target, and became the preferred pre-loaded round. Two other pieces of equipment used for the first time in combat were TOGS and the GPS system. All users of TOGS declared it a battle winner, especially against the Iraqi armour which had (if it was lucky) first generation infra-red viewing equipment, which was no match for TOGS. The TOGS system proved to have an even longer effective range than the US thermal system employed on the M1A1. The use of the Global Positioning Systems (GPS) was also a major step forward and while only available at the time to command tanks, it was the best desert navigation system ever used up to that time. It allowed senior officers to command from the leading elements. Prior to the use of GPS, navigation in the desert was by sun compass and stars, not exactly ideal for a modern fast moving armoured division.

Perhaps the most celebrated event for Challenger 1 in Operation Granby, and one that buried the ghosts of CAT 87 was the engagement of a moving T-55 by the CO's tank Royal Scots Dragoon Guards. Lieutenant-Colonel Sharples' gunner spotted a T-55, obtained a range by laser and fired... and achieved a first round hit. Nothing out of the ordinary there, apart from the fact that the engagement range was over 5 kilometres, which went down in tank lore as the longest ranged tank to tank engagement (although Challenger could fire out to 10 kilometres in an indirect fire role), this was gunnery at its best and luckiest. The Challenger 1 came home in March 1991 to Germany partially vindicated. As Major-General Patrick Cordingly aptly stated upon his return from the Gulf, " the Challenger is a fighting tank, not a competition tank".

Tanks of the Queen's Royal Irish Hussars wait on the docks in November 1990. It would be over 2 months before they would see action. [DL]

A Challenger waiting for its desert modifications with turret trained aft. [DL]

Peacekeeping in the Balkans

Despite its excellent performance in Operation Granby, the Challenger 1 came home to an uncertain future, and was due to be replaced starting in 1998 by the Challenger 2, which had been delayed by Vickers Defence Systems' total commitment to supporting Operation Granby. The Challenger 2's availability date had also slipped so that the production vehicles could incorporate the recent lessons learnt from Operation Granby. The number of Challenger 2s required was still being debated when the Challenger 1 again received the call to arms. In 1992 the republics comprising the former state of Yugoslavia erupted in violence, with each faction committing genocidal atrocities, and the United Nations could not sit idly by. In Operation Grapple a small brigade-sized British peacekeeping element was deployed to support the United Nations with Warrior MICVs with its base at Split in Croatia. High hopes for a quick resolution to the local conflicts were naturally held, but due to the UN's rigid rules of engagement the United Nations Protection Force (UNPROFOR) proved rather toothless against persistently aggressive local factions. Several incidents involving UN troops being held as hostages or being used as human shields by Serb and Croat forces (as well as ethnic cleansing incidents) caused outrage in the western media. Ultimately it was recognized that a more decisive intervention in the Balkans was necessary.

The peacekeeping operation was handed over to NATO in December 1995 under the guise of IFOR (Implementation Force), and as part of the UK's contribution (known as Operation Resolute) was to deploy mechanized infantry forces supported by Challenger 1s from the 7th Armoured Brigade in a British-led multinational division (South-West) based on Banja Luka. Initially IFOR represented a potent menace to all transgressing factions, giving out the message that if you messed with IFOR you messed with the big boys. The factions were stunned by the robust response from NATO forces when any breaches occurred, but some still did try to argue. One such incident near Banja Luka in 1996 involved a T-55 crew who ignored IFOR orders not to move until given permission, and drove around a road bend and up a track only to be met face to face by a loaded Challenger 1. The result was that the T-55 retreated back in quick order. It was strange to see 62

A Challenger 1 being guided into the hold of a container ship in Split, Croatia, following its service with SFOR. It has been cleaned of all personal equipment for the voyage back to British Forces Germany, as loading space was very tight. [PH]

Challenger 1s awaiting loading at Split in Croatia after service with SFOR. It was realised that eventually the need for a main battle tank on the SFOR mission would diminish as the threat level declined and lighter forces could carry out patrol duties. [PH]

A very clean Challenger 1 in the markings of a unit serving with KFOR, taken in an arena in the UK, at a military show. [SP]

The King's Royal Hussars in Bosnia in 1997. The Challenger 1 was a good machine to show the warring Balkan factions that NATO meant business. The ROMOR reactive armour array on this tank is still in Operation Granby colours. [KRH]

A Challenger 1 on patrol in the snowy scenery of Bosnia-Herzegovina, during the days of the IFOR mandate. Notice the meeting of two eras; the modern main battle tank and the millennia-old horse and cart. For a long time during and after the conflict in the Balkans, the horse and cart were the only mode of transport for many local inhabitants. [Army]

A Challenger 1 of the Queens Own Hussars in Bosnia, on patrol enforcing the IFOR mandate. Notice the coiled and stowed inter-vehicle slave lead on the glacis, to the right of the driver. This was used to supply power to vehicles with dead batteries or to the tank itself, and was used in the same manner as car jumper cables. [PH]

A Challenger 1 unloading from the container ship at Split in Croatia, ready for service with IFOR. The crew have strapped their bedroll mats onto the side of the turret. The Challenger was not so well equipped with stowage bins as its predecessor the Chieftain. [DT]

A Challenger 1 from the Queens Dragoon Guards loading onto a container ship, of note is the suitcase on the rear decks and the collection of flags the tank is flying. For a time the flying of national flags was banned on NATO vehicles during the IFOR mandate, but eventually the practice crept back in and was a source of national pride to the crews. [Sgt. B. Gavin USA]

The Royal Scots Dragoon Guards' commanding officer's Challenger 1, seen in the hangars at the Bus Station Mrkonjic Grad in Bosnia. The Scottish Saltire (flag) can be just seen on the front left side of the turret. [RG]

tons of Challenger replete with ROMOR ERA and Chobham side armour arrays rumbling through the countryside doing patrols which might normally be expected to be carried out by CVR(T) Scimitar, but in the early days IFOR needed to dominate, which it did very well. The Royal Scots Dragoon Guards, Queen's Royal Hussars, The 1st Queens Dragoon Guards and The King's Royal Hussars all deployed squadron sized forces of Challenger 1s to the Banja-Luka, Mrconij Grad and Birachi areas during the next few years.

When the mandate switched from IFOR to that of SFOR in late 1996, the Challengers did not have to patrol as much but they were still available at short notice if needed. The SFOR

With typical British Tank crew humour, "Dennis The Menace" a well-known character from British comics, appeared on the side of one of the Royal Scots Dragoon Guards' Challenger 1s in Bosnia. [RG]

Challengers were a strong reminder of NATO's resolve, especially during local elections, and one night while on duty on communications I received a call from the Brigadier that crashed all our Challengers and Chieftain support vehicles out, almost on a war footing. The reality of keeping peace was that the NATO forces throughout the Balkans had to be ready at a moment's notice to use overwhelming force. Even in the ruins of Bosnia-Herzegovina humour still could be found in simple situations. I was working with the Royal Scots Dragoon Guards from their base in the former bus terminals at Mrconij Grad, and it was policy for the commanding officer's Challenger to go on patrol flying the Scottish flag. One day it had gone out and we were awaiting its return (which you could hear long before you could see), when in the middle of the road a lone, brave policeman stood with his speed camera. The Challenger

A Challenger 1, CVR(T] Sultan and Challenger Armoured Recovery Vehicle (initially nicknamed a Rhino] line up on the occasion of the handing over of the garrison at Mrkonjic Grad in Bosnia from the Royal Scots Dragoon Guards to the Kings Own Hussars in 1997. [RG]

A Challenger 1 makes its way slowly through a town during the IFOR mandate. Tanks became a very common sight in those days and were almost accepted as normal, they conveyed the image to the former warring factions that NATO would take no nonsense. [Army]

A Challenger 1 on patrol in Bosnia as part of IFOR, notice the prominent display of the Union Flag. This had been banned during the UNPROFOR mandate as it was considered provocative, but a policy of flag bearing was rapidly adopted by the all the NATO troops. Notice the spent artillery cases in the foreground. [Army]

saw him and carried on and drove past him leaving one baffled policeman, wondering why the tank did not stop so he could ticket it. The King's Royal Hussars relieved their last Challenger 1 squadron in December 1999 from Mrconij Grad, ending the Challenger 1's final combat deployment.

Al Hussein

Once the Challenger 1s were pulled back from the Balkans in 1999 their days in British service were numbered, and the Challenger 2 had already been accepted into service with the British Army as a single type replacement for all Challenger 1 MBTs on the 25th July 1998. The Challenger 1 was slowly phased out of service by 2000 as the Challenger 2s passed their reliability tests and were accepted into the RAC, and a decision had to be taken on what to do with them. The Kingdom of Jordan had strong ties to Great Britain and had been searching for a means to upgrade their armoured forces for some time, and the Challenger 1 offered a degree of commonality with the Khalid MBT already in service. In the end a controversial sale to Jordan of 288 Challenger 1s had been quietly negotiated in March 1999, at rock bottom prices (with £1 per tank being quoted). The MoD defended this decision against substantial media criticism, saying the Challengers were only worth scrap value to Britain, although the cost of the spares package that accompanied the purchase ran into the millions of pounds sterling.

This Jordanian Al-Hussein has been modified to represent some proposed upgrades as an alternative to the Falcon, which include the fitting of the Swiss RUAG 120mm compact smooth bore gun, and fitting of Raytheon IFCS to replace the original British fire control system. The tank is known as "the Hybrid". Also visible in the picture is a mock-up of an independent commander's viewer with thermal capability, and the turret bustle, which contains the Claverham load-assist system to aid the loader. A new NBC pack and different auxiliary generator are also proposed. If this tank was to enter service it will give the Jordanian army a very potent weapon. [Internet]

The Jordanian Challenger Falcon demonstrator firing on a desert range. The shot was taken with a high speed camera, as the flight of the projectile can clearly be seen. [BW]

A second transfer of 100 more Challenger 1s to Jordan was approved in October 2002 at no cost. This removed all but 30 of the Challenger 1 gun tank fleet from the British inventory, with a very few vehicles being gifted to museums while at least one prototype and a Mk.3 (94KC37) have ended up in private ownership. Several more are used as training aids, thus still serving their country. There ends the story of Challenger 1 in British service, a mixed series of events from hopeful inception, through humiliation at CAT87, to vindication in Operation Granby and beyond. The Challenger was renamed the Al Hussein in Royal Jordanian Army service, where it joined its predecessor the Khalid. The heirs of the Shir 1 and Shir 2 designs found themselves not in Persia, nor in Britain, but in the service of King Abdullah's army.

The Al Hussein was evaluated for considerable upgrades to meet the threats in its new environment, where potential enemies theoretically included Israel and Syria. The sale of the Challenger 1 to Jordan included a large quantity of 120mm ammunition but no depleted uranium munitions could be included, and while stocks of British 120mm munitions are substantial, Jordan has expressed the desire to eventually convert their Al Husseins to the more common NATO 120mm smoothbore weapon. The main upgrades considered for the Al Hussein all center around the turret. Options evaluated included re-equipping the original Challenger turret with the 120mm RUAG L50 (a Swiss development of the Rheinmetal 120mm smoothbore), an additional layer of frontal armour and a Raytheon fire control system. This upgrade was called the Hybrid Turret and was developed by the King Abdullah II Design and Development Bureau in 2003.

A second and more expensive option was to re-turret the Challenger hull with the Jordanian designed Falcon turret. The Falcon turret is a 120mm L50 RUAG smoothbore-armed two-man turret with automatic loading and ultra-modern stabilized panoramic thermal sights. Its narrow frontal profile makes it a very hard target to hit hull down and it features advanced armour protection, quite possibly derived from the Chobham system. The Falcon turret system has thus far been developed through 3 different marks and is compatible with other MBTs like the M60 that are also operated by Jordan's army. Ultimately

A good view of the Jordanian Challenger Falcon showing its very futuristic layout, with a hatch each side of the gun for commander and gunner. [Internet]

funding has not yet appeared to enable the upgrading of the Jordanian Al-Hussein fleet, but even as these vehicles stand in their original British configuration they represent amongst the most powerful MBTs in service in the Middle East.

The Challenger 1 Main Battle Tank remains in many eyes a misunderstood weapon procured at a very controversial period in Britain's recent history, a tank accepted by the army against the backdrop of economic decline. The Challenger 1 was a Cold War weapon built in Thatcher's Britain, and its evolution was affected by foreign events ranging from the fall of the Shah, the shift in defence priorities as a result of the Falklands War and the continued fulfilment of Britain's NATO obligations. The Challenger 1 must be remembered as a tank developed to foreign requirements and adopted by Britain for political reasons. The Challenger 1 was not the army's first choice for a Chieftain replacement and was never bought in numbers sufficient to replace the Chieftain. Eventually however the Challenger 1 was adapted to the RAC's satisfaction. It was a tank that proved very effective in the test of war, however imperfect it may have earlier seemed in the eyes of peacetime warriors.

The Challenger Armoured Repair and Recovery Vehicle

Only one Challenger 1 variant was selected for production, largely because earlier Chieftain based bridgelayers, and specialised engineers vehicles were seen as adequate to fulfil the army's

Some of the best improvised frontal armour you can get, simply add the dozer blade, and voila instant spaced armour! The hydraulically operated dozer blade was fitted to one tank per Squadron, usually the second in command's tank. It was useful for digging in, and for general low key dozer duties, and it also would provide some limited armour protection. [DL]

The dozer blade fitting from the right side, showing how neat and tidy the conversion is, and also how much simpler than that fitted to the Chieftain. Dozer tanks in Operation Granby naturally enough did not receive the front ROMOR ERA frame. [DL]

A three-quarter front view of the dozer blade attachment, this one seen fitted prior to Operation Granby. Quite often the dozer blades were not fitted by units as they could cause problems if they experienced failures, being left in the hangars unused, which happened all the time with the Chieftain. [DL]

needs during the 1980s and after the end of the Cold War. During the early years of the Challenger 1's service the regiments equipped with the new tank relied on Chieftain variants for all support tasks, including armoured recovery. The Chieftain ARV Mk.7 was a capable vehicle with a greater reserve of power than that available to the Chieftain gun tank because it had a higher power to weight ration made possible without the weight of a gun turret or heavy armour. Nonetheless, while the Chieftain ARV served the Challenger regiments' recovery needs during the 1980s, a dedicated armoured recovery vehicle based on the Challenger hull and powertrain offered far greater potential as a recovery vehicle. Vickers began studying a Challenger recovery

A closeup of the dozer fit on the hull front of the Challenger. Normally one tank per squadron received the dozer kit. [DL]

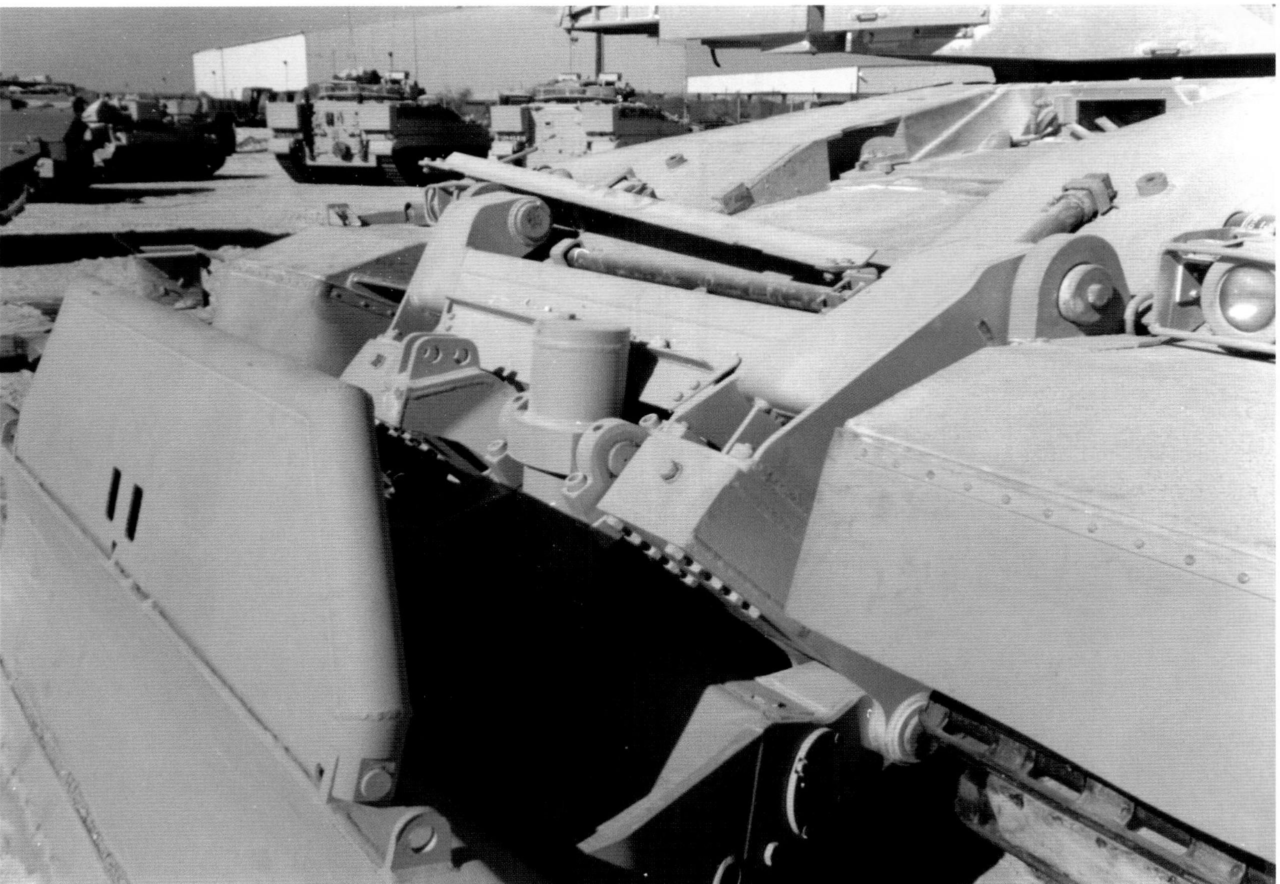

This shows some of the hydraulics behind the dozer blade. [DL]

variant as soon as the gun tank was introduced into service and was issued a contract for 30 Challenger based ARVs in 1985. These were accorded a lower priority than the gun tanks and the first vehicles of this contract did not appear until 1990.

The Challenger 1 recovery vehicle was originally known as the Rhino, but is officially referred to by the acronym CRARRV (ChallengeR Armoured Repair and Recovery Vehicle). It carries a 7.62mm GPMG for self-defence and is armoured with conventional welded steel armour. It is powered by the same standard power pack as the gun tank. It is equipped with a main 52-ton winch that (by means of pulleys) can be used to pull over 104 tons. The vehicle's auxiliary winch is used for secondary tasks not associated with MBT recovery. The CRARRV's Atlas crane can lift 6.5 tons enabling power pack changes for the main battle

Until 1990, the British Army relied on the Chieftain ARV and the venerable Centurion ARV Mk.2 for its heavy recovery needs. Of these the Chieftain ARV was tasked with recovering the Royal Armoured Corps' Chieftain and Challenger Main Battle Tanks, while the Centurion ARV Mk.2 was used by the Royal Engineers, who retained Centurion based special purpose vehicles until Operation Granby was concluded. Here we can see the newly arrived Challenger CRARRV (then nicknamed Rhino) on the left, the old Centurion in the center and the Chieftain ARV on the right. The photo was taken in late 1990 in Saudi Arabia during the buildup for the liberation of Kuwait. [DL]

The Chieftain ARV was an adequate design but lacked a large reserve of power for dealing with the heavier Challenger MBT, and the CRARRV is a far more powerful vehicle that has now served for nearly 25 years. [DL]

tank and any lighter armoured vehicles almost anywhere. The CRARRV can be equipped with a special wheeled trailer to enable carrying a complete Perkins 1200 HP CV-12 Challenger MBT powerpack or 2 Warrior MICV power packs across country, although vehicle speed is naturally reduced when towing the trailer. The Challenger 1 MBT was normally pulled with drawbars but could also be towed with hawsers if necessary.

The first 4 Challenger CRARRVs were rushed into service for Operation Granby, where the Chieftain ARV Mk.7 was still standard equipment in the armoured regiments for the duration. Baptised *Faith, Hope, Charity* and *Big Geordie* (the last after the Vickers Newcastle plant where they were built), these vehicles quickly proved their worth supporting the 4th Mechanized and 7th Armoured Brigades. Following Operation Granby a further 44 CRARRVs were ordered to replace all other British Army heavy armoured recovery vehicles. One CRARRV was issued to the Squadron Fitter Section of each of the 3 sabre squadrons of each armoured regiment as deliveries permitted in the first half of the 1990s. When Oman ordered the Challenger 2 to replace its Chieftains in 1993 4 new built CRARRVs were

The front mounted blade is employed to brace the CRARRV during heavy recoveries employing the vehicle's front winch. At first only 4 CRARRVs were sent to the 7th Armoured Brigade in the gulf, and they received the names *Faith, Hope, Charity* and *Big Geordie.* [DL]

Call Sign 30 Bravo, *Big Geordie* readies for the ground war in Operation Granby. The Challenger Armoured Repair and Recovery Vehicle was a huge success and completely replaced the Chieftain ARVs in a very short time once the troops came home from Kuwait. [DL]

The massive bulk of the CRARRV seen from the rear three quarter. [DL]

A CRARRV of the SCOTS DG scraping out an emplacement with its blade, Saudi Arabia 1991. [DL]

A top view of a CRARRV on the docks in Saudi Arabia showing the rear smoke dischargers and engine decks, as well as the large Atlas recovery crane. [DL]

bought with the first 18 of 28 MBTs. Oman is the only foreign user of the CRARRV.

The CRARRV accompanied the Challenger 1 gun tank to BATUS, to the former Yugoslavia and of course to British Forces Germany for the remainder of the Challenger 1's service life. When the Challenger 2 was introduced in 1999, the CRARRV was retained as the standard armoured recovery vehicle for the new tank, following it to Kosovo that same year, and to Iraq in 2003. During Operation Telic in 2003 the CRARRV saw extensive service under enemy fire for the first time. The SCOTS DG's battlegroup advanced into Iraq on March 22nd 2003, beginning nearly 4 months in the combat zone. The SCOTS DG's tour included several incidents where the regiment's CRARRVs proved their value and the skill and bravery of their crews against determined enemy resistance and difficult terrain. The area around Shatt al Basra included a number of embankments and narrow

Not the usual customer: A CRARRV recovers an M1A1 Abrams. [DL]

Mabel, a CRARRV employed by the SCOTS DG. Eventually every Challenger regiment received 3 CRARRVs. [DL]

Big Geordie from the front three quarter with blade raised. The markings carried by this CRARRV still look quite pristine, so we can imagine that this photo was also taken before the ground war got into full swing. [DL]

raised roadways that proved difficult to navigate at night and the B Squadron commander's tank had to be recovered after shedding a track on March 23rd 2003.

A far more dangerous rescue involving the recovery of a severely bogged Challenger 2 of C Squadron SCOTS DG near Abu Al-Khasib occurred on the night of March 29th 2003. The Challenger 2 in question had lost both tracks maneuvering at night on a narrow causeway and had been blasted with 2 direct ATGM hits and over 20 RPG hits. Only after repeated attempts lasting 9 hours were two CRARRVs able to pull the tank to safety under enemy machine gun and RPG fire. The stranded Challenger 2 was returned to service two days later after its optics were replaced, a testament to the effectiveness of Chobham armour and the skill of the fitters. During the recovery both CRARRVs had snapped their main winch cables and had operated at great risk to their crews. The 2nd Royal Tank Regiment and Queen's Royal Lancers were both also equipped with the CRARRV during Operation Telic.

In subsequent Operation Telic deployments to Basra area the CRRARVs have been provided with substantial modular armour upgrades (including bar armour) similar to those employed on the Warrior and Bulldog MICVs to reduce the threat of RPGs and with new tracks of the same pattern employed on the Challenger 2. Much of the armoured role in Iraq became one of patrolling by individual armoured troops, and remotely detonated IED weapons became the greatest threat to British vehicles. With the end of the British military presence in Iraq, it is expected that the CRARRV will serve for many years to come alongside the small Challenger 2 MBT fleet being retained by the British Army. It is one of the world's most powerful recovery vehicles and in the past 24 years has consistently proven its excellence in the field.

Big Geordie **with the front dozer blade fully lowered as it would be in a winching operation. [DL]**

Bosnia was the next deployment, and here we can see a CRARRV with Union Jack prominently flying in the Balkans on one of the NATO peacekeeping missions. [DL]

Ihis shows one of the four sets of Multi barrel smoke grenade dischargers fitted to the CRARRV. Below them one of the fuel filler
caps can be seen and to the left (with a black rubber cover fitted) is
he mount for the Amber rotary light. [R. Griffin]

Located on the front right wing are the three external fire extinguisher handles, and as can be seen by the signs, each one is for a
specific area on the vehicle. [R. Griffin]

he front right block of smoke grenade dischargers, and located below is a hand held fire extinguisher. Note that is encased in green plastic cover, this is to hide it's colour (which in keeping with EU law has to be post box red, not the best choice for a combat vehicle). [R. Griffin

Looking from right to left in the foreground is one of the hydraulic arms that raise and lower the blade, behind that can be seen the pulley block used to increase the pull. [R. Griffin]

This is the rear of the blade, and we can see just how solid items on an armoured vehicle are, no room for soft plates here. [R. Griffin]

Head on view with the driver hatch open to the right (looking from rear) and his periscopes visible. Either side of the picture can be seen the hydraulic pistons that support and raise and lower the blade. [R. Griffin]

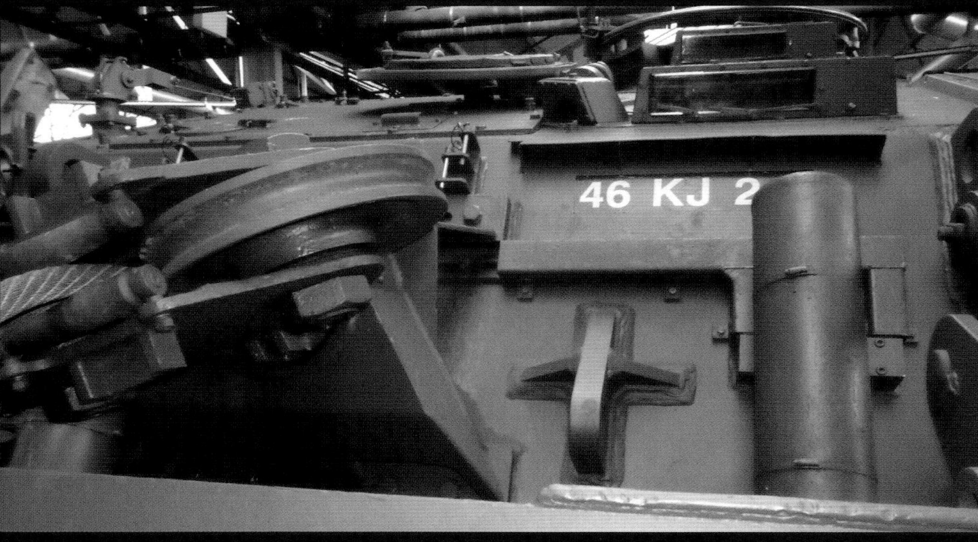

The drivers station and the pulley block. [R. Griffin]

The winch rope is a substantial cable, secured when not in use. We can also see the left bank of smoke dischargers under the lighting cluster. [R. Griffin]

The left side fire extinguisher in its tactical plastic cover, and the three external handles mirrored from the right side. It does not matter which side a crewman exits: he will always be near an extinguisher handle if needed. [R. Griffin]

A close up of the extinguisher and its cover, notice the quick release clip retaining it. [R. Griffin]

View showing some of the large grills that the CRARRV has to aid cooling and as air intakes. [R. Griffin]

Spare track links are carried on the hull, although for some reason this vehicle has the old single pin track links carried even though it is actually fitted with the new double pin track introduced on the Challenger 2. [R. Griffin]

In this view we can see the air intake for the vehicle NBC system, this is a similar fitting to that found on later marks of Chieftain. [R. Griffin]

Here we can see the location of the exhaust, set into one of the stowage bins. Note the rubber bungs hanging out the vertical face of the stowage bin, when in this position they allow any water that may have collected in the bin to drain away. [R. Griffin]

In this view we can see how the crane hook weight is stored on the rear hull wall, also visible is another set of smoke grenade dischargers. [R. Griffin]

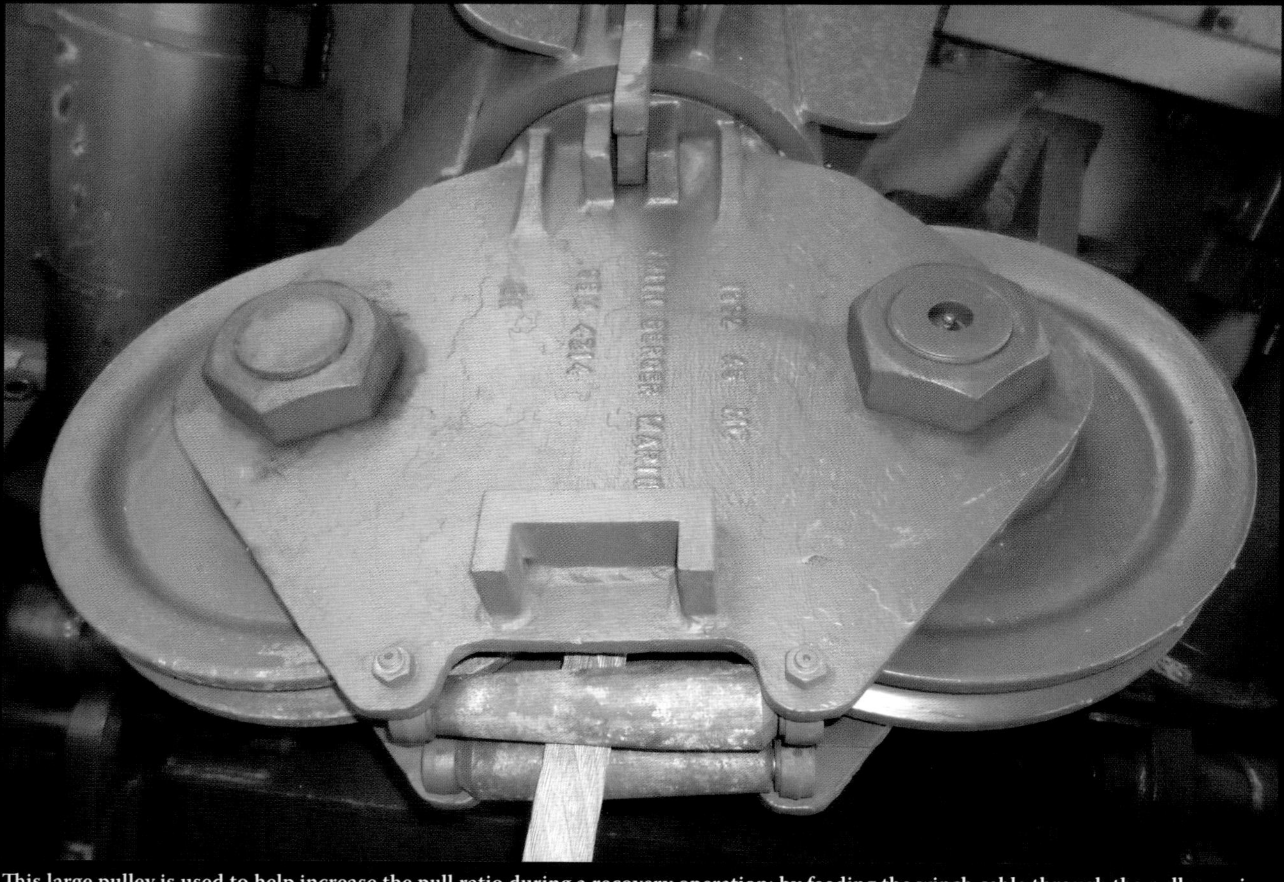

This large pulley is used to help increase the pull ratio during a recovery operation; by feeding the winch cable through the pulley various ratios can be achieved. [R. Griffin]

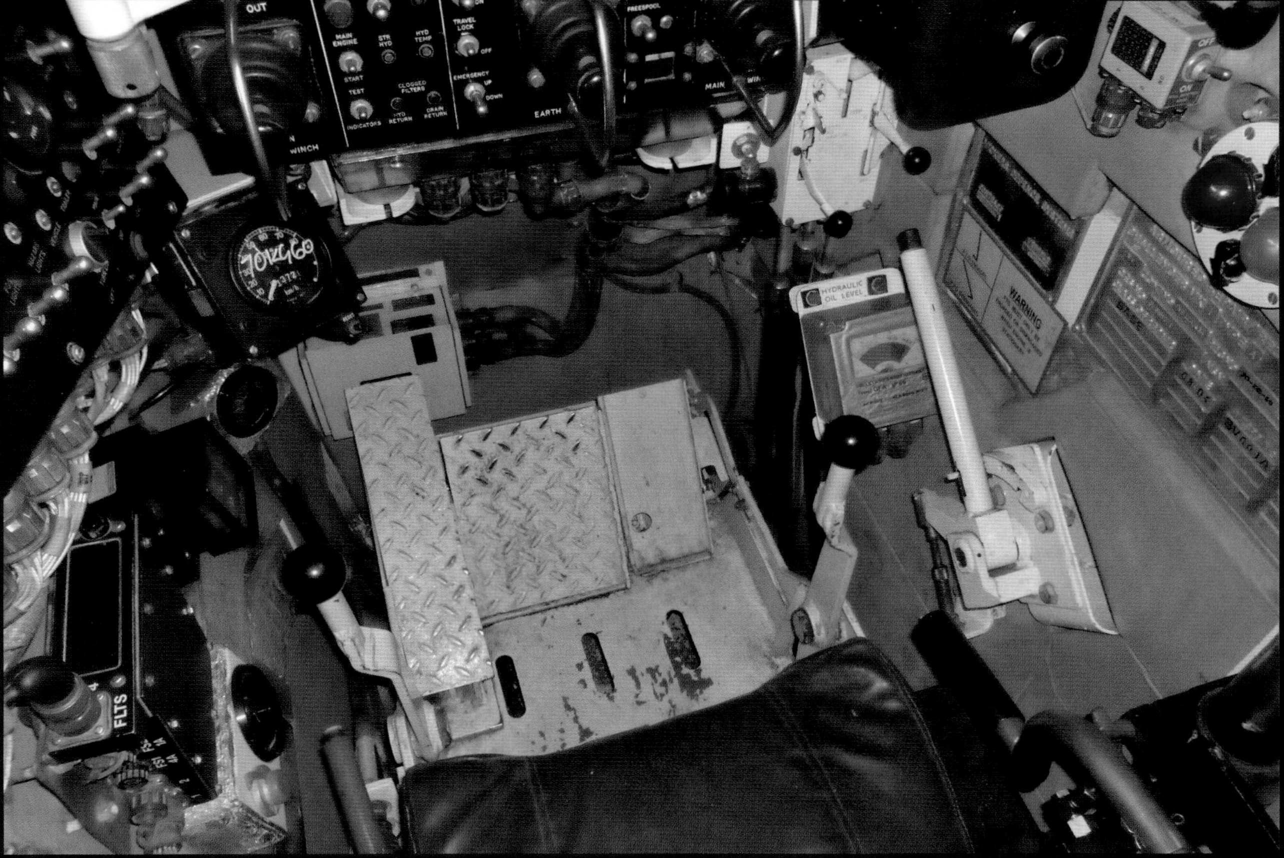

A general view into the drivers cab showing most of the normal day to day controls, the rectangular aluminium plate on the right wall gives the vehicle details including when it has been to workshops. [R. Griffin]

Left view of drivers controls, located on the left is the main panel giving him most of the information he needs on the vehicle such as RPM, temperature and all the lights. [R. Griffin]

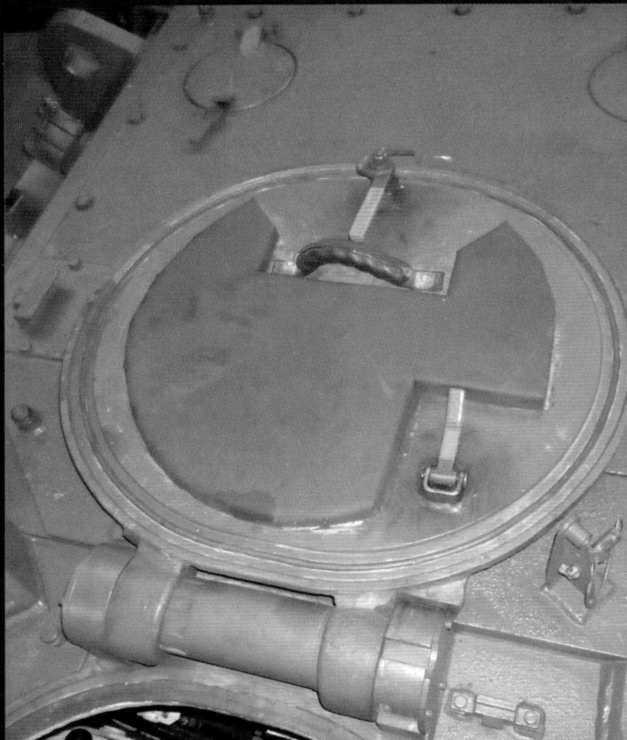

Inside view of one of the hatches, of note is the very simple and uncluttered method of securing the hatch once closed, also note the red painted handles, most hatch handles are painted red on AFVs for high visibility. [R. Griffin]

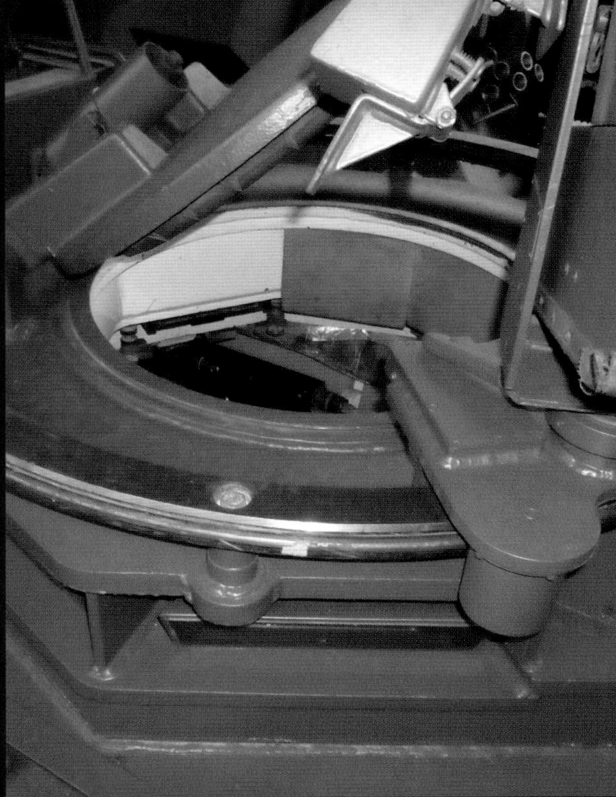

The vehicle commander's cupola with the mounting for the 7.62mm GPMG visible on the right of the picture. [R. Griffin]

The machine gun mount fitted to the cupola, as can be seen it is almost identical to the loaders machine gun mount on the Challenger 2 MBT. [R. Griffin]

The commanders hatch, showing the single red painted locking handle. The cupola is very simple on the CRARRV, and the commander has to stand to fire the GPMG (which is not ideal).

The Commander's GPMG mount showing on the right side the retaining lip for a box of 200 7.62mm rounds and on the left the link exit chute.

One of the Bowman Radio system antenna bases. Compared to the Clansman radio bases it has no rubber mounting, and depends on the large spring to give it flexibility when the antenna hits overhanging obstacles such as tree limbs. [R. Griffin]

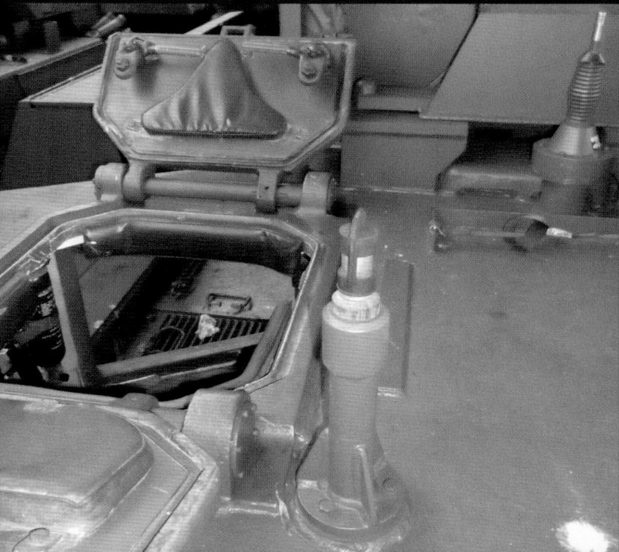

On the left of this picture is one of the access hatches to the inside of the CRARRV. The hatches bear more than a passing resemblance to those on the loaders station on the Chieftain MBT. In the foreground, the short stubby mounting with a rubber cap is for the location of an amber rotary light. [R. Griffin]

Close up of the crew hatch showing the thin rubber bump protection located between the twin locking handles. [R. Griffin]

This shows the other crew hatch and their obvious Chieftain parentage. Note the webbing strap at the top which is used to help pull the hatch shut. [R. Griffin]

This shows some of the hydraulic pipes and the hand control for the crane. [R. Griffin]

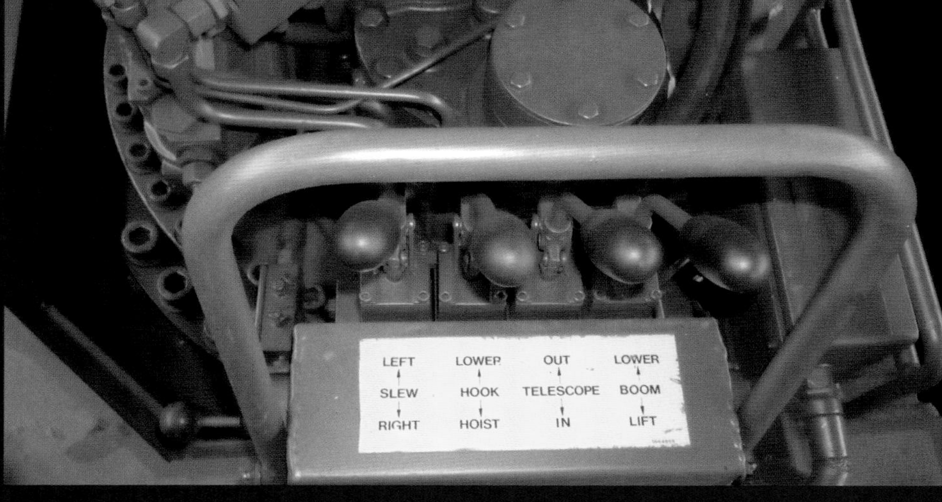

The yellow plate has very clear instructions telling the crane operator what each handle controls. [R. Griffin]

Looking forward along the vehicle's right hand side, visible are the crane and the stowage bins and basket. Normally these would be full of equipment. [R. Griffin]

Twin hatches giving access to the crew compartment. If required, the CRARRV can accommodate a full 4 man Challenger crew in addition to its own three man crew. [R. Griffin]

The crane with the lift warning sign in yellow on its side and one of the main engine exhausts. [R. Griffin]

A close up of the warning limits sign, this tells the crew how much weight can be safely lifted (and at what boom length) with the Atlas crane.

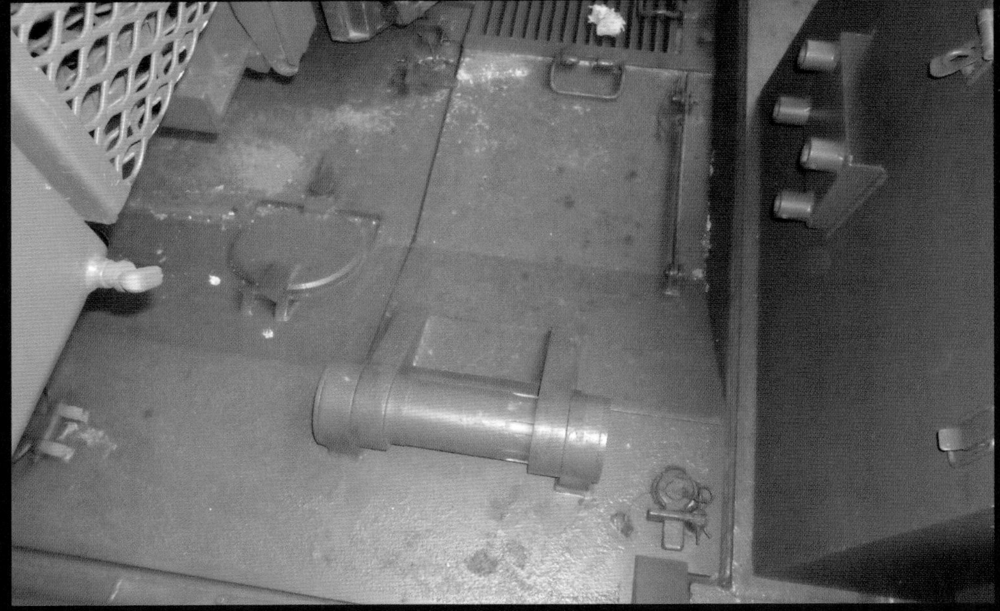

One of the many access pannels on the engine decks on the CRARRV, of note is the substantial thickness of the hinges. [R. Griffin]

The right hand side engine and transmission decks, with the transmission decking being in the background. [R. Griffin]

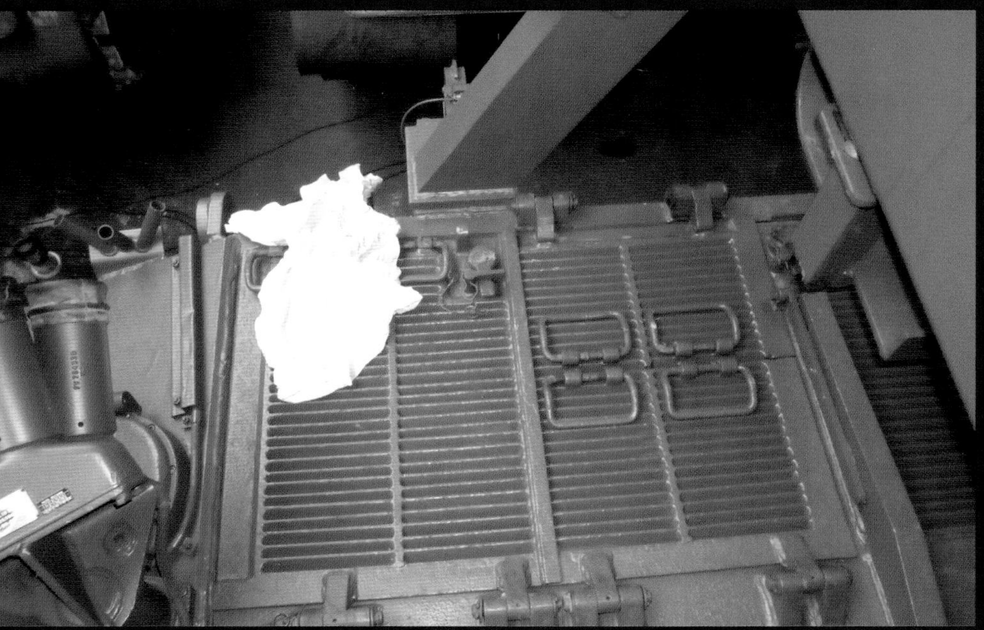

A close up of the transmission decks, also visible to the left of the decks the three mounting tubes for the carbon fibre poles that are part of the camouflage net system. The mounting tubes are locate on all four corners, and when the poles are assembled and placed in them they form a very large gazebo like shape, over which the camouflage net can be draped. [R. Griffin]

Visible is the rear of one the storage bins, transmissi decks, a cleaning rag, smol dischargers, camouflage po tubes and the mount for ar other amber rotary ligh [R. Griffin]

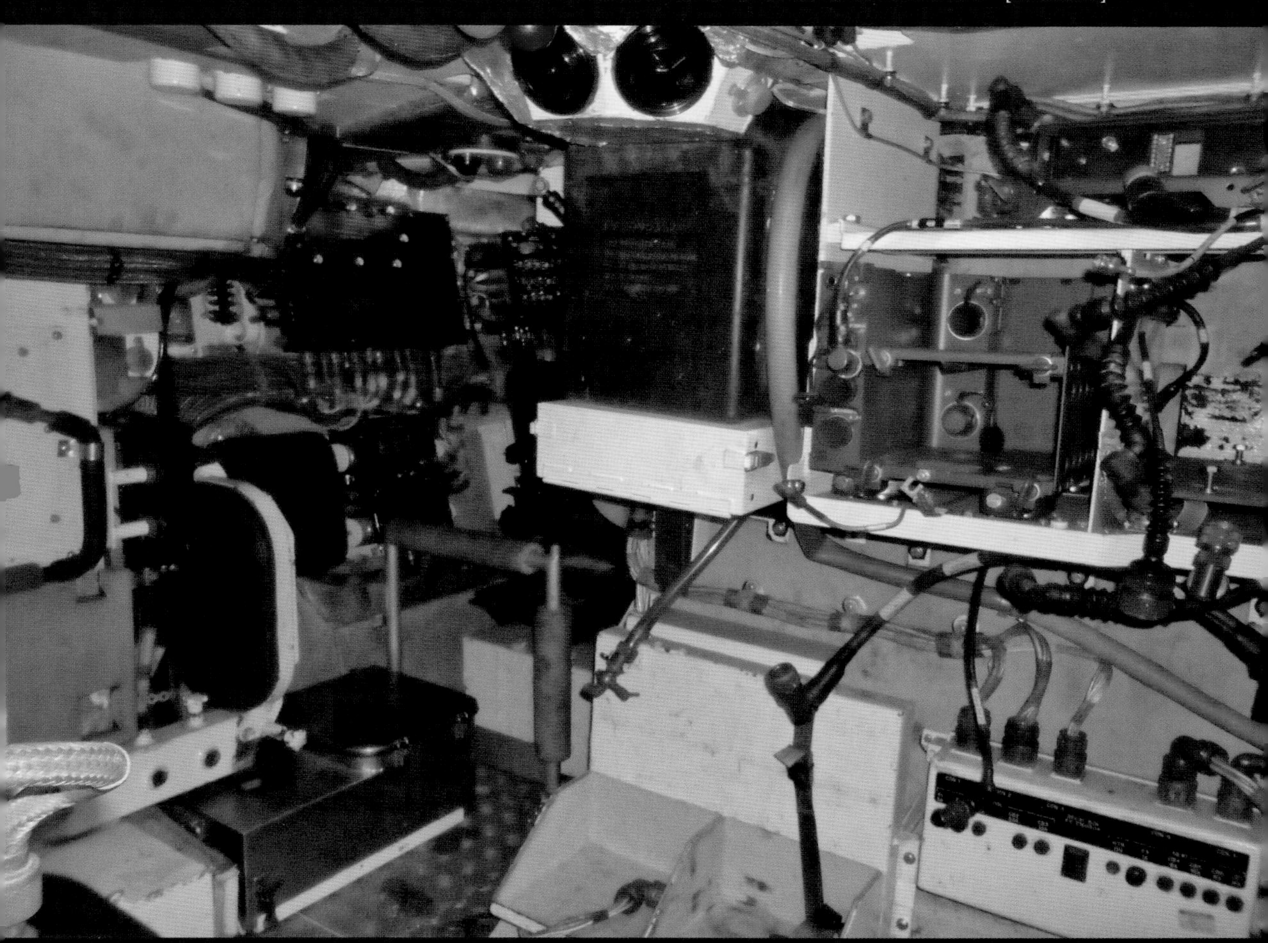

A view inside the crew compartment, the green empty boxes are mounts for the Bowman radios, the blue pipe is part of the internal drin ng water system. [R. Griffin]

General view of the crew compartment roof with the drivers hatch, the commander's cupola and crane controls all visible. Note this vehicle does not have the GPMG mount fitted. [R. Griffin]

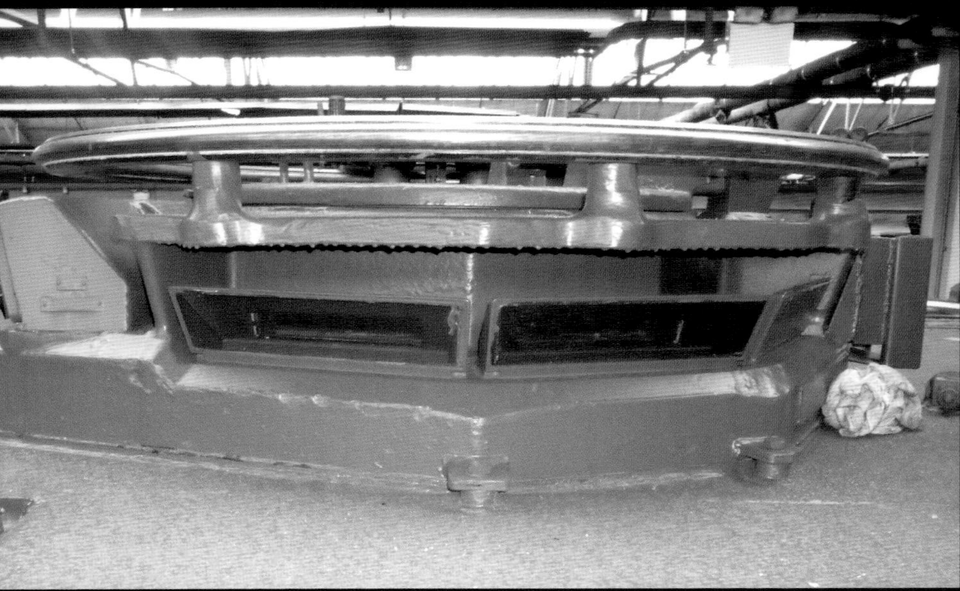

Two of the periscopes from the commander's cupola. Notice how basic this is compared to what would be fitted to an MBT. No wiper system is fitted to these. [R. Griffin]

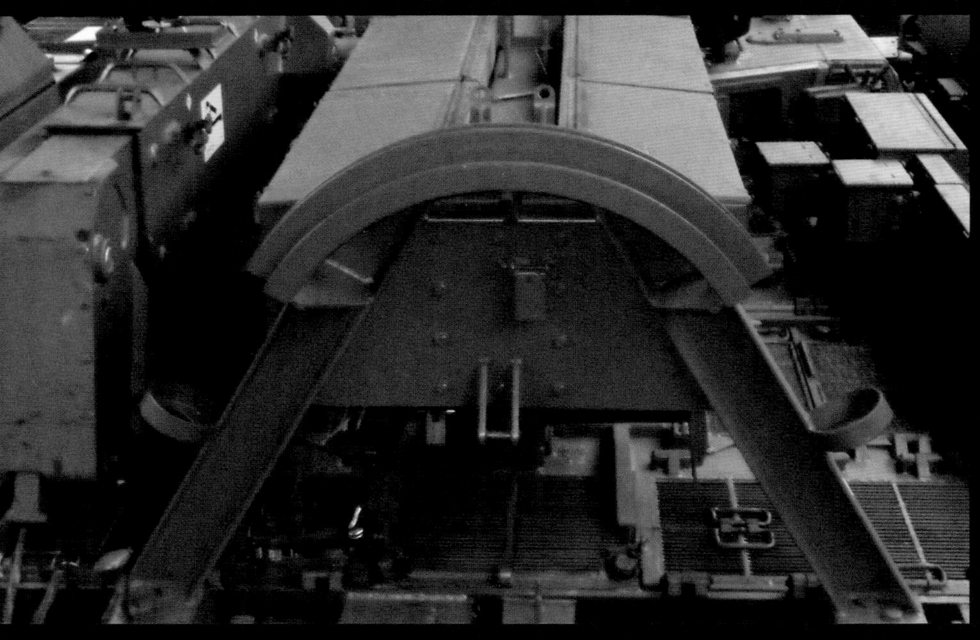

Rear view showing the crane on the left and the bulk of the rear stowage boxes. [R. Griffin]

The commander's cupola, showing the traverse bed for the machine gun, which is the CRARRV's only armament. The main part of the mount is not fitted here, but the base and locking/control handle can be clearly seen. [R. Griffin]

Left view looking forward on an up-armoured CRARRV, notice how the extra plates are located to the hull.The trough ¾ of the way down would contain more armour add on pannels when the vehicle deployed. [R. Griffin]

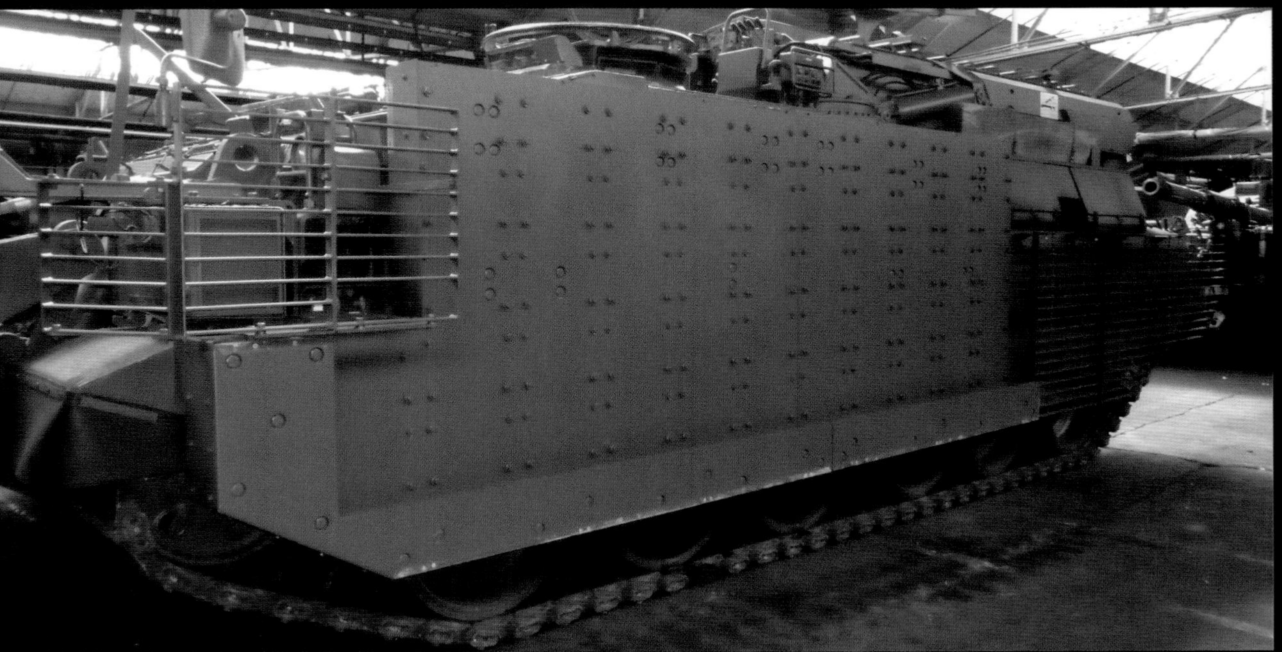

A view showing the large amount of extra armour carried by the CRARRV when it is operational. The trough running down the side of the vertical plates is for more add-on armour. This modular approach allows the armour arrays to be configured to suit the CRARRV's mission. [R. Griffin]

A close up showing how the bar armour is fitted to the hull. [R. Griffin]

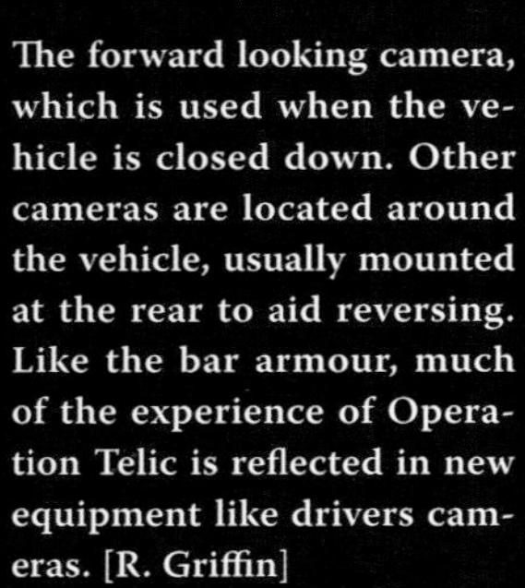

The forward looking camera, which is used when the vehicle is closed down. Other cameras are located around the vehicle, usually mounted at the rear to aid reversing. Like the bar armour, much of the experience of Operation Telic is reflected in new equipment like drivers cameras. [R. Griffin]

This is part of the new anti-IED electronic equipment which minimizes the threat of remotely detonated mines and other explosives. [R. Griffin]

Right front bar armour protection, with the Chobham armour panels visible in the background on the left. Bar armour is an anti-hollow charge protection system above all, and is most useful in stopping RPG projectiles. [R. Griffin]

Seen clearly in the centre is the screen that the driver uses when driving on cameras, a great step forward from periscopes. [R. Griffin]

Top view showing the attachment of the bar armour screen and how it all fits to the hull. [R. Griffin]

Good view showing the bar armour attachments, IED box, camouflage pole locations and the left hand hydraulics for the dozer blade. [R. Griffin]

Left rear light cluster and also how the holebone recovery bars are secured to the hull. [R. Griffin]

Another view showing the bars secured, note also the green cross on the vehicle first aid box. [R. Griffin]

Centre towing attachment, of interest is how thick it is and how much weld there is to ensure that it is secure. [R. Griffin]

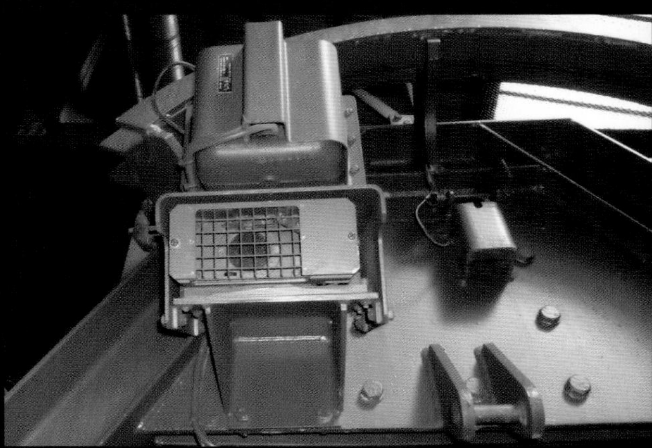

The rear mounted camera and IED box. [R. Griffin]

Operation Granby Challenger 1 Mk.3: Modifications for the First Gulf War

A good view of the right side appliqué armour array fitted for Operation Granby. The side pannels provided Chobham protection to the vehicle's suspension and more importantly, to the ammunition stored below the turret ring. [DL]

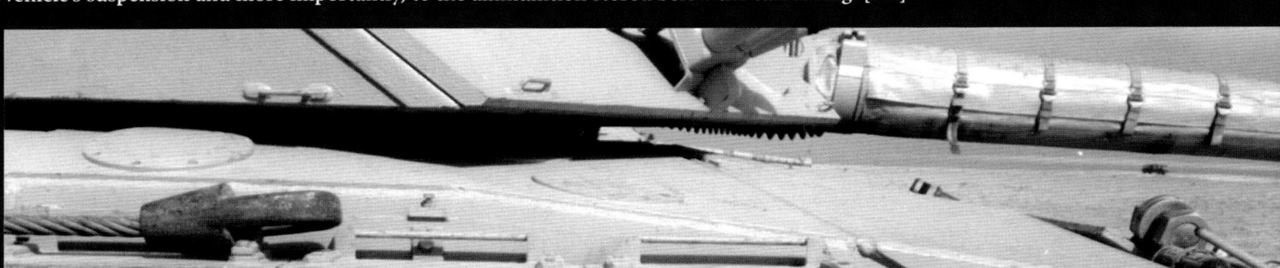

Another view of the side armour panels. [DL]

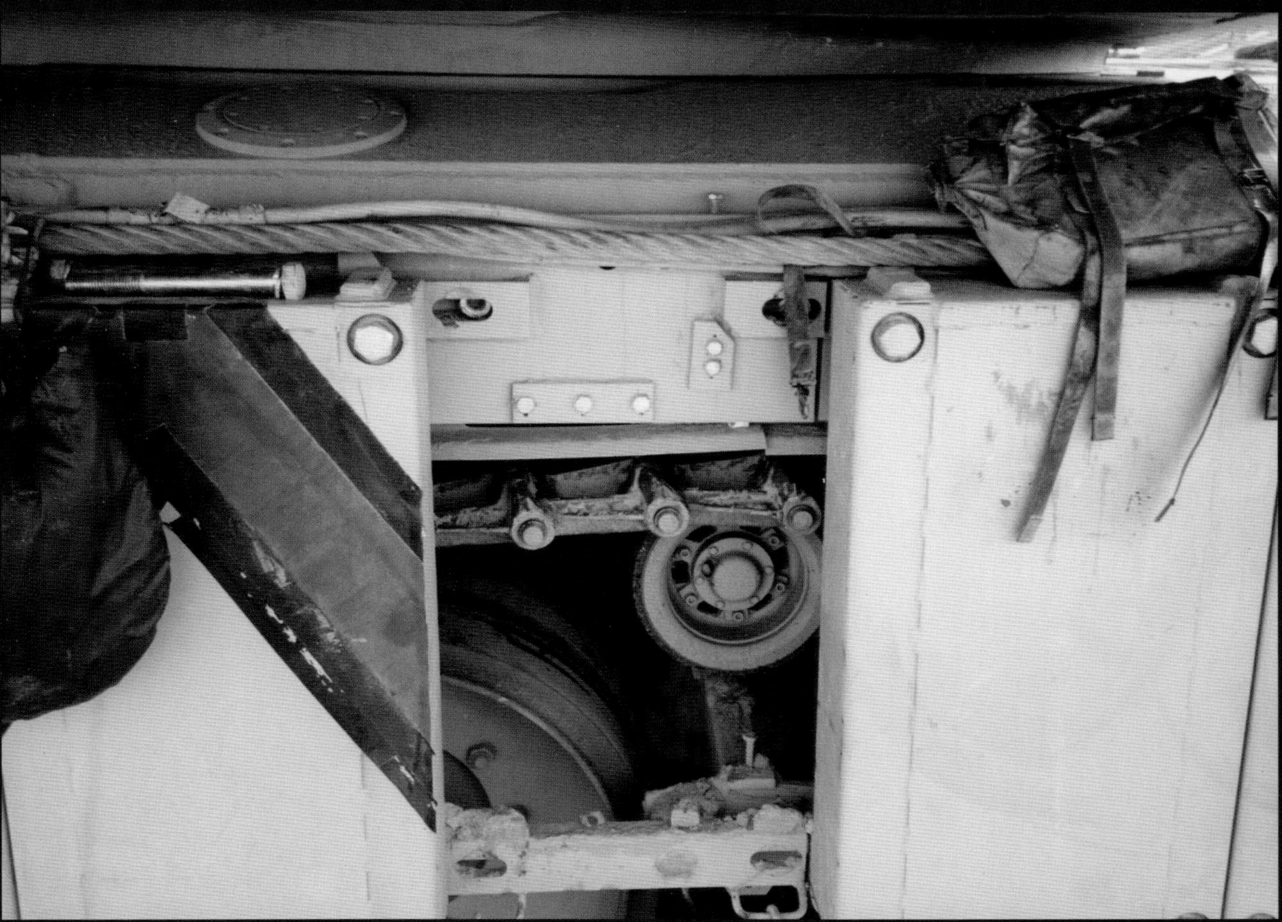

The individual appliqué Chobham armour side plates could be lowered to carry out day to day maintenance on the Challenger's suspension. The photograph also gives a very good idea of the thickness of the add-on blocks. [DL]

The left side Chobham armour plates seen from the front ¾. [DL]

We can see here that the front section of the side armour, which covered the area inside the hull where ammunition was stored and where the turret basket was located, was thicker than the aft panel. [DL]

A side view of the armour array fitted to the left side of a Challenger 1 Mk.3 for Operation Granby. [DL]

As part of the armour upgrade the towing ropes were relocated to the tops of the side armour array panels. [DL]

The side armour arrays could be lowered to access the suspension, which needed plenty of maintenance in desert operations and with the extra weight of amour carried. [DL]

Rear view of the modifications carried out to the rear hull of a Challenger 1 during the buildup to Operation Granby. The vehicle range was increased significantly by the 400 extra litres of diesel fuel which could be pumped into the main fuel tanks by a small pump carried between the two drums. The vehicle call sign was typically painted on the rear fuel drums. [DL]

Another view of the right side of a Challenger 1 from the 4th Mechanised Brigade during Operation Granby. The improvised stowage provisions that were adopted almost universally for Operation Granby included the use of Ferret and Chieftain stowage bins reclaimed from decommisioned vehicles. The turret and hull (though not on the vehicle shown] also received numerous racks for jerrycans. Many of these stowage "improvements" remained on the Challengers until the end of their service lives, though the supplementary armour packages were returned to ordnance at the end of the war. [DL]

e 200 liter fuel drums fitted to the rear of the 1st UK Armoured Division's Challengers prior to Operation Granby. [DL]

side view of a fuel drum fit on the rear of a Challenger 1 in the gulf. In the background is a Chieftain ARV, up to then the main armoured

A good rear view of a Challenger 1, showing the brackets for external fuel drums. Also visible are parts to make up an "A" frame towi bar. The long horizontal bar is one leg (the other will come from another tank] the large component at the bottom is the tow bar attach to the dead tank while the coupling is the small part with three holes seen at the top. [DL]

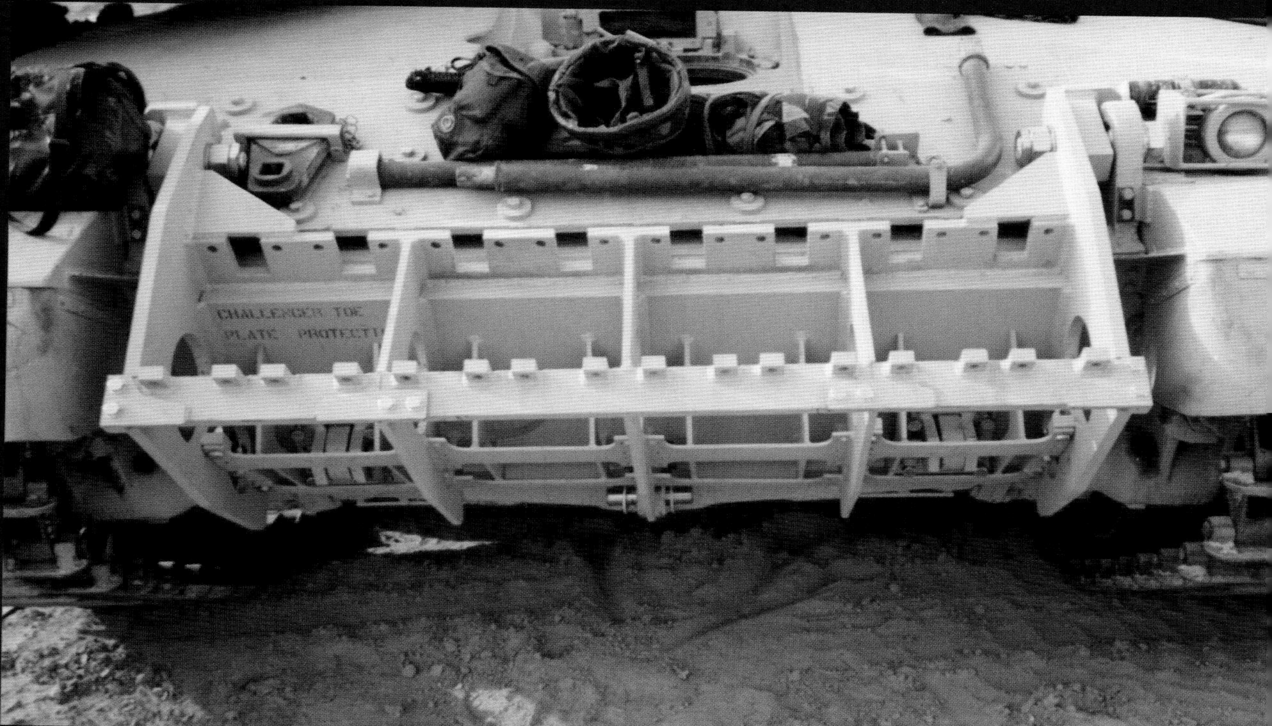

The ROMOR cradle fitted to Challenger 1's bow armour to carry the Explosive Reactive Armour blocks. This shows very well how it wa fitted and could be an inspiration for a modeller's diorama. The right angle bar and the large hexagonal socket by its side are the trac adjuster, these would be fitted to the large nut on the idler wheel [illegible]ket and using its ratchet action the tension on the track could [illegible]

Kit, clobber and the substantially built but empty frame fitted to the Challenger's lower glacis, ready to accept the Explosive Reactive Armour bricks which provided an extra level of protection to the Challenger's lower front. [DL]

A photograph showing the front of a Challenger 1, perhaps taken after the end of Operation Granby in 1991. On the frontal ROMOR pack can be seen two of the crews' tank helmets, which are worn over the headsets inside the tank, and plenty of crushed soft drink cans. [DL]

Above the ROMOR ERA in its heavy frame, a sheet of spaced armour was bolted to the Challenger's glacis plate. Frontally, with the additional armour in place, these modifications would have made the Challenger's hull immune to almost all hostile threats on the battlefield, except heavy mines. The upper glacis and turret front required no reinforcements because the Challenger had been designed to fight hull down on the European battlefield and no Chobham armour was fitted to the lower front plate. [DL]

Jerry can racks, a very common addition to Operation Granby Challengers. These have been added to the turret rear right, but many tanks had them welded onto the side arrays as well. [DL]

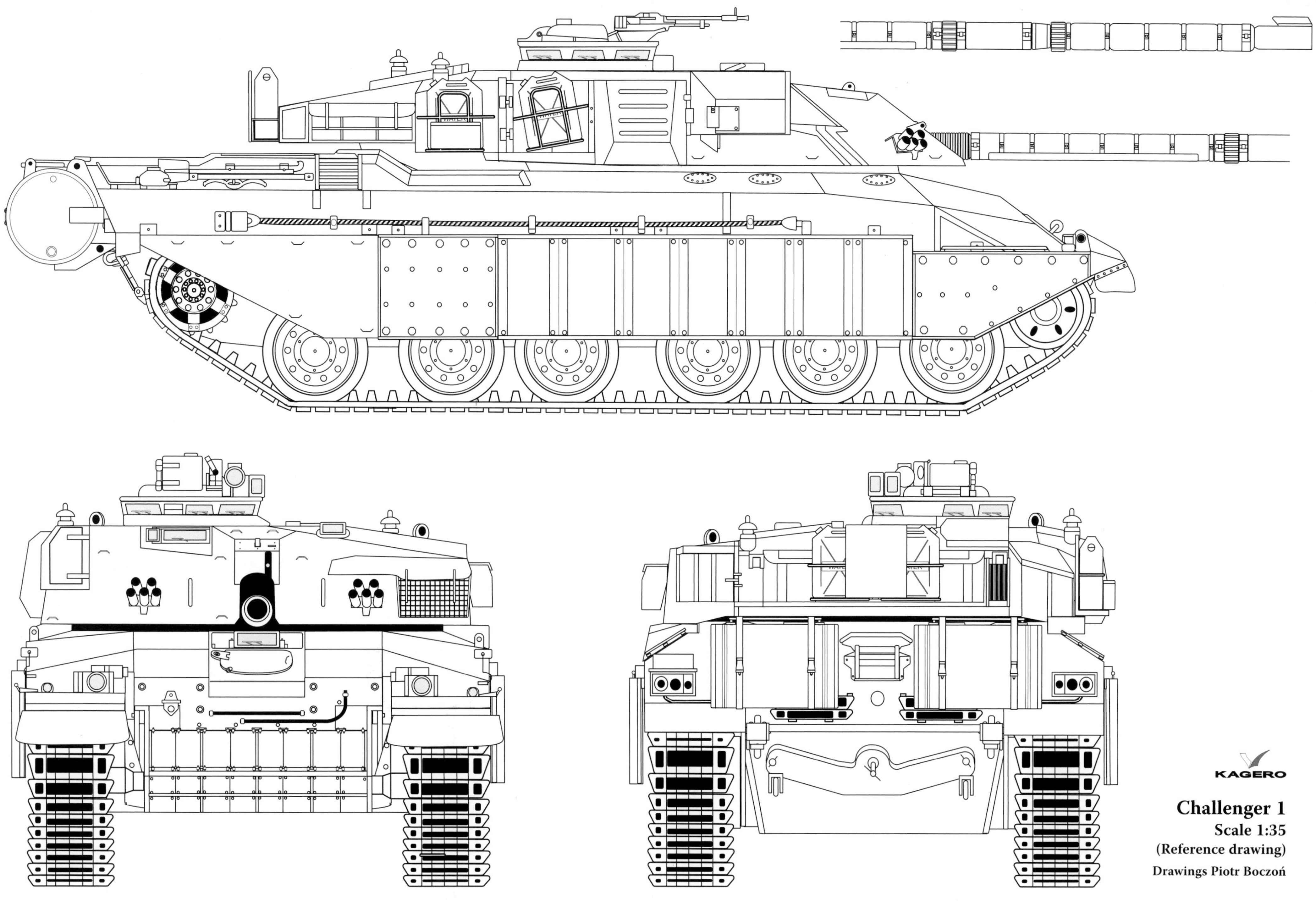
KAGERO
Challenger 1
Scale 1:35
(Reference drawing)
Drawings Piotr Boczoń

KAGERO

Challenger 1
Scale 1:35
(Reference drawing)
Drawings Piotr Boczoń

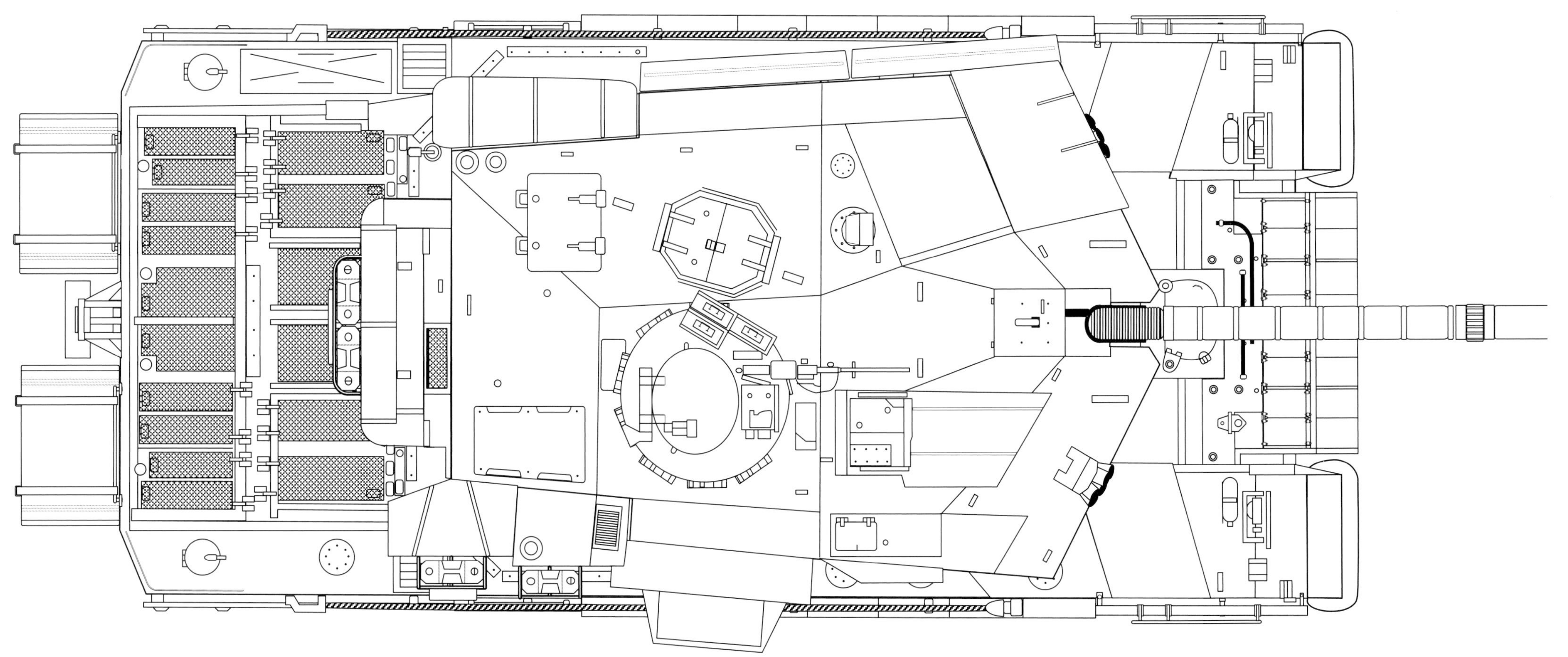

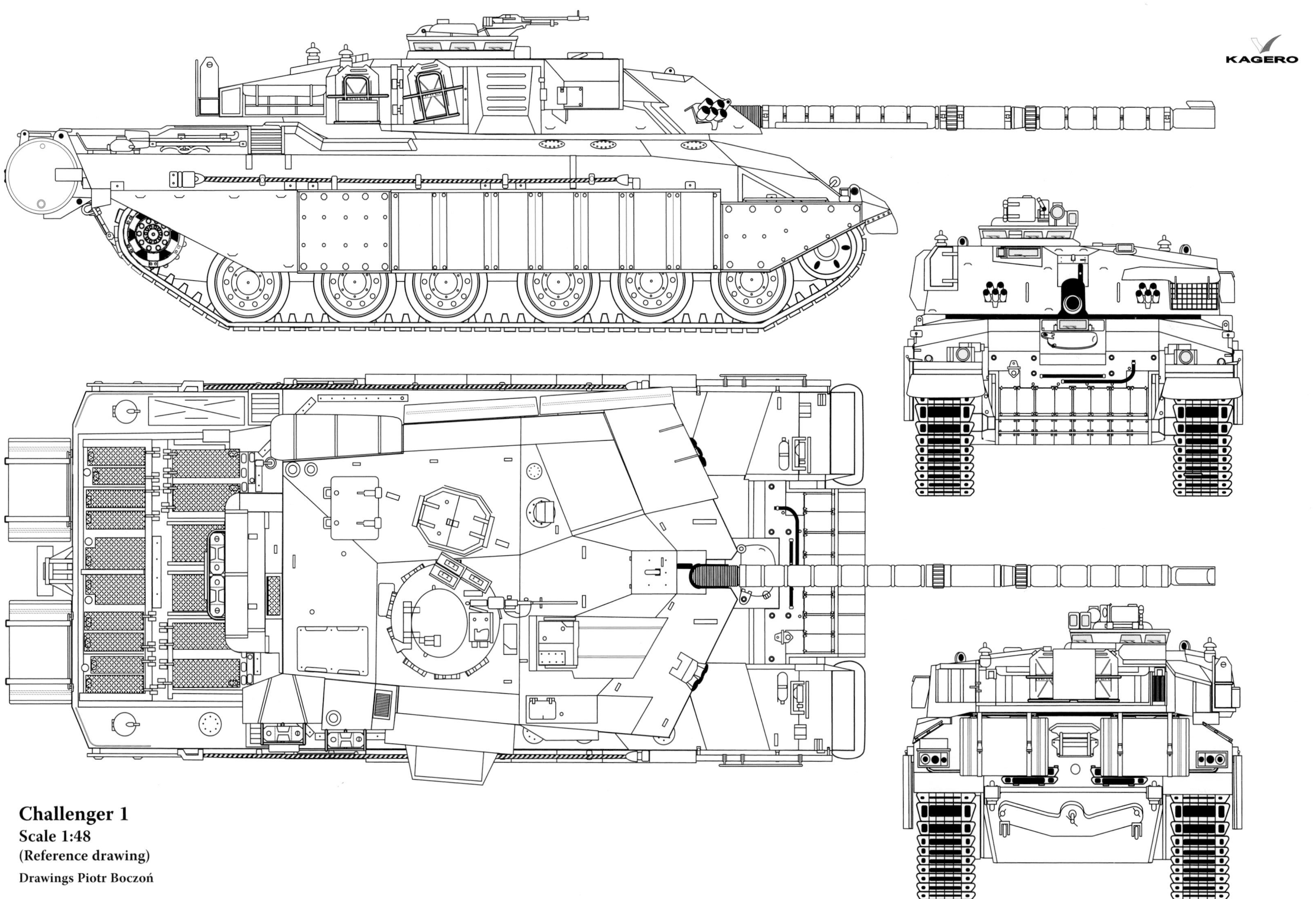
KAGERO
Challenger 1
Scale 1:48
(Reference drawing)
Drawings Piotr Boczoń

Painted by Sławomir Zajączkowski

36 KA 53 Challenger 1 Mk.2 *Dark Angel*, D Squadron The Royal Dragoon Guards, OPFOR Demonstration Squadron, School of Infantry, Warminster, UK, 1994:

36 KA 53 was an OPFOR vehicle at the Land Warfare School (formerly the School of Infantry) on Salisbury Plain in the mid-1990s. Its rather sinister name *Dark Angel*, along with the grim reaper stylised into the stencil, met with a certain amount of official disapproval and eventually by all reports the vehicle name had to be repainted in a less macabre manner. The BATUS-like paint scheme worn by the OPFOR was to differentiate its vehicles from the black and NATO Green vehicles of visiting units training at Warminster.

ARDUS, Call Sign 20 A Squadron, 14/20th Hussars, 4th Mechanised Brigade, 1st UK Armoured Division, Operation Granby February 1991:

A fine example of the extemporised markings applied by some crews during Operation Granby is ARDUS of the 14/20th Hussars, most probably a Challenger 1 Mk.3. Besides the black jerboa of the 4th Mechanised Brigade on both turret sides (on the right side this would have been carried on the side of the TOGS barbette), the old cap badge of the 20th Hussars is carried on the door of the TOGS barbette. The 14/20th Hussars features several tanks with decorations applied to the frontal ROMOR armour arrays. The field postage address of the 14/20th Hussars is carried on the side armour along with a high visibility, if somewhat rough rendition of the A squadron triangle.

Painted by Sławomir Zajączkowski

Call Sign 10, A Squadron King's Royal Hussars Challenger 1 Mk.3, NATO SFOR, Bosnia 1997:
The King's Royal Hussars was formed in 1992 as an amalgamation of The Royal Hussars and the 14/20th Hussars as the British Army was reduced in size under Options for Change. The KRH deployed to Bosnia from June to December 1997 and again from June to December 1999 as part of SFOR. The tank depicted wears a mixture of repainted and original Operation Granby scheme supplementary armour, which was typical for the period. The KRH regimental crest over a maroon-yellow-maroon background was worn on the TOGS barbette door and the crew have secured their bedrolls to the large wire mesh cage fixed to the turret side.

Call Sign 22, A Squadron, 1st Queen's Dragoon Guards, NATO KFOR, Kosovo August 1999:
The 1st Queen's Dragoon Guards were late comers to the Challenger 1, receiving the type after Operation Granby for Operation Resolute in Bosnia. In what must have been one of the last deployments of the Challenger 1 in British service, A Squadron of the 1st Dragoon Guards deployed to Kosovo in August 1999 for six months before being converted back to a formation reconnaissance regiment equipped with CVRT light tracked AFVs in 2000.

Painted by Sławomir Zajączkowski

Call Sign 22B, Royal Scots Dragoon Guards, 7th Armoured Brigade, 1st UK Armoured Division, Operation Granby February 1991:
The SCOTS DG was the second armoured regiment of the 7th Armoured Brigade, and carried the Scottish Saltire on its vehicles, along with white call signs. The red jerboa was usually worn on the front of the TOGS barbette but as with most Operation Granby vehicles, the hurried repainting prior to leaving Germany meant that unit markings were reapplied by the tank crews themselves (with plenty of variation as a result). The crew of this vehicle added its own typical personal touches, with jerry can racks on the turret side and on the hull side Chobham armour arrays. They have also spray painted their postal details on the extra ammunition boxes attached to the turret side mesh basket in order to increase the vehicle stowage.

Desperate, 64 KG 91 Call Sign 30, B Squadron, The Queen's Royal Hussars, 2nd Canadian Multi National Brigade, NATO IFOR, Bosnia, January 1996:
The Queen's Royal Hussars was formed in 1993 from the amalgamation of the Queen's Royal Irish Hussars and The Royal Hussars. It was the first Challenger 1 regiment deployed to Bosnia and served in the 2nd Canadian Multi National Brigade, receiving a Canadian Forces Unit Commendation for its service, the first time such a commendation was ever made to a non-Canadian unit. It was also the first foreign unit citation won by a British regiment since the Korean War.

Painted by Sławomir Zajączkowski

St Davids, 64 KG 83, Call Sign 0B, D Squadron, The 1st Queen's Dragoon Guards, NATO SFOR, Bosnia 1996:
The D Squadron Commander's tank seen during the continuation mandate of the original IFOR deployment, implemented by NATO following the failure of the UNPROFOR peace keeping effort in the former Yugoslavia. The tank pictured carried the Welsh Dragon emblem on the side of the TOGS barbette on the right hand side of the turret in addition to the QDG crest worn on a red background on the TOGS barbette door. The 1st Queen's Dragoon Guards are nicknamed the Welsh Cavalry.

By 2012, the Al-Hussein had served its first 10 years in Jordan and has proven to be a reliable weapon system capable of considerable upgrading should funding become available. The modernization of the Al-Hussein fleet may be conducted with South African cooperation in future, as both Jordan and South Africa have agreed to a shared military technology arrangement, starting with the program codenamed MERLIN. Jordan has hosted a number of large exercises with U.S. and British participation in recent years, including exercise Eager Lion 2011 and 2012. The Al-Hussein pictured carries markings seen at the 2012 exercise, including the gun barrel partly wrapped in red cloth or plastic for the exercise.

KAGERO.EU

Shop online shop.kagero.pl

AMX-30 CHAR DE BATAILLE 1966-2006

New releases. Coming soon!

Messerschmitt Me 262 Schwalbe vol. II

Japanese Heavy Cruiser Takao 1937–1946

Junkers Ju 87 D/G vol. I

Pz.Kpfw. V PANTHER

READ FOR FREE on KAGERO's Area

LIST OF PUBLICATION SERIES

TopColors

miniTopColors

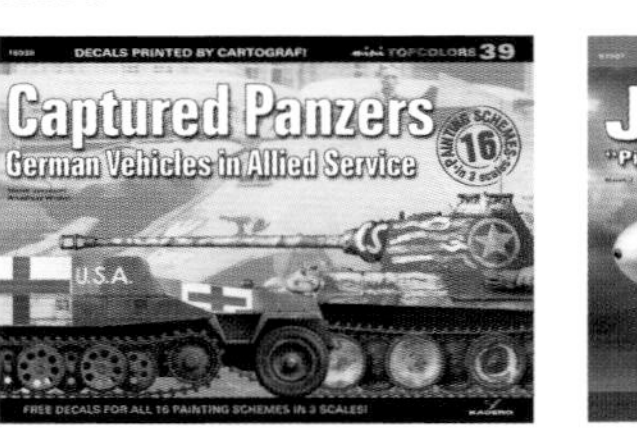

Units

TopDrawings

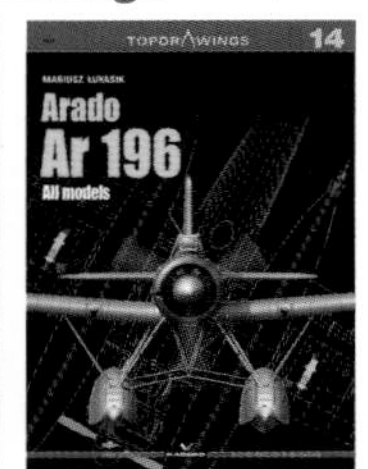

Legends of Aviation

Legends of Aviation in 3D

SMI Library

Photosniper

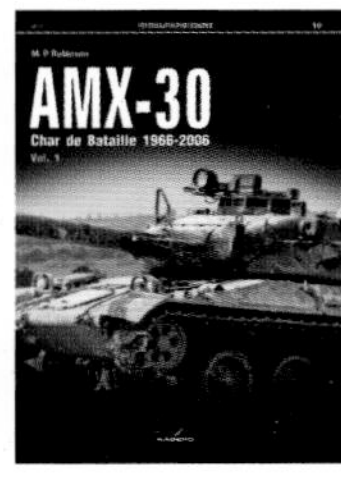

Monographs / 3D

Air Battles

Super Drawings in 3D

www.shop.kagero.pl

phone +4881 501 21 05